THE SECRET TO ALL THINGS FRANCHISING

How franchising is the secret to a life of passion, purpose and prosperity

Compiled by

Linda Ballesteros

The Secret To All Things Franchising

How franchising is the secret to a life of passion, purpose and prosperity

As You Wish Publishing, LLC
Connect@asyouwishpublishing.com

ISBN-13: 978-1-951131-15-9

Library of Congress Control Number: 2021902835

Printed in the United States of America.

Nothing in this book or any affiliations with this book is a substitute for medical or psychological help. If you are needing help please seek it.

Table of Contents

Foreword

Sabrina Wall

Sometimes life happens to you instead of you planning the path. For me and franchising, that is exactly how our love story began. I was not looking to start a franchise, but I met a few people who owned a franchise. They were not sophisticated. They were young. They were a little rough around the edges, but they were smart, and they were scrappy. I was really amazed they owned a franchise together. Two young guys not coming from much who together owned a franchise with employees and accounts they managed. That is where the idea of owning a franchise started for me. If they can do it, I can do it too.

"If they can do it, I can do it too," is one of the most important and empowering phrases one can say to themselves. It is the comment that begins a legacy. It requires confidence and practicality. With it, so many amazing things have occurred.

In 1954, Roger Bannister broke the record for the four-minute mile. Many thought it was impossible prior to his achievement. After he did it, hundreds of runners achieved that time and better. There is something that happens when people see others achieving something. They think to themselves, "If he can do it, I can do it." I have heard this same phrase so many times in my professional franchise career when franchise buyers are interviewing current franchise owners to see what their experience has been like. After that interview, they will report back to me, "If they can do it, I can do it." And that is the honest truth. You can do it. It's been done. You were designed to achieve success, too, and you can do it. If you pick the right system, follow it, and use the support available—you can do this. We often say at the Franchise Brokers Association, "With the right tools and teams, you can be exceptional." Franchising done well makes that happen.

During the interviews with franchise owners, these franchise buyers hear the incredible success stories of what *good* franchises help the franchise owners create. I talk to millionaires every day in the franchise space because the model helps take the load off the owners so they can be freed up to do the roles they are exceptional at. That may be leading, managing, marketing, or operational procedures. Different franchises complement different people and bring out the best in those people. You have to find the franchise that brings out the best in you.

Taking a step back, I said earlier that I fell in love with franchising. That is the truth. I jumped headfirst into franchising because I discovered with great delight that anyone who wanted it, and had a few years of good financial decision making, could become a franchise owner. I discovered this because I started a franchise at the same time that I became a franchise broker.

For those of you who don't know who franchise brokers are, Franchise brokers are similar to real estate agents. They help franchise buyers find, vet, fund, and own a franchise. As a franchise broker, I was completely astonished by how many low-cost franchises were available to the average person. I came into the business thinking most franchises cost over a million dollars, and they were all food concepts. But once in the business, I learned the huge variety of franchises.

There were franchises ranging from pet supplies to window cleaning. There were franchises in vacation rentals to manufacturing services, from children's education to executive coaching. There were franchises in every industry you can imagine and at every price range. This was so inspiring. I felt completely empowered to change people's lives by helping them to discover and then own a franchise and get the true independence they desired.

Franchising is a very unique segment of the business. It allows people with an entrepreneurial and independence-minded spirit to start a business, learn the ropes, and reduce their risk. The franchise owner essentially partners with the franchise system, and they share work between them. This makes it easier for the franchise owner to scale and grow the business because they are not in charge of every component of running it.

Because of this, franchising is ideal for those people who don't want to become a slave to their business, those who want to scale quickly, and for those who want to have a higher probability of succeeding as a business owner. That is, if the selection of the franchise is done properly upfront.

I found early on that all franchises are *not* created equal, and the huge variety in the quality of the systems was remarkable. Some systems are so well refined, they have five people to call on for every unique need the franchise owner has. Other systems don't offer an inkling of support and misrepresent their offer. It is critically important to do proper research in the investigative process before purchasing a franchise.

Franchising is governed by the Federal Trade Commission (FTC), a consumer protection agency. Franchise systems must provide any prospective purchaser of a franchise with a franchise disclosure document before they purchase. This document is amazing. It tells you the whole track record, experience level, and past performance of the franchise system. For those skilled in reading them, a franchise disclosure document can show the business model of the franchise system, the retention rate of franchise owners in the system, the profitability of the franchise and the franchise owners running locations, as well as a wealth of additional information about the viability of the system. This document is packed full of insightful information and can help a franchise buyer gain tremendous clarity before they purchase the franchise. It can help them make smart investment decisions.

However, most people don't understand what they are reading. They don't get a franchise attorney who does understand it to review it, and they don't know what to look for to uncover these key facts. As a result, people buy franchises that aren't good systems or aren't good systems for them. **We do not want that to be you.** A *good* franchise for one person may be a terrible franchise for another. Just like you wouldn't put a shy financial analyst in a sales position, you have to find franchises that fit your talents in order to be successful with it.

In this book, we have brought together a collection of franchise professionals to help you on your journey to find, vet, fund, and own a franchise. They will share their experiences from the field, help arm you with basic knowledge about franchising, as well as powerful insights to make the best franchise decision, and finally, help you with tips to run your franchise most successfully.

When done right, with a strong team around you, you really can be exceptional as a franchise and business owner. That's why we always tell people, "With the right tools and teams, you can be exceptional." Remember that. It's the truth. Now, let's find you the right tools and teams. Your future of independence is waiting for you around the corner. This book will help you have the confidence to own it.

Sabrina Wall, CEO

Franchise Broker Association

https://www.franchiseba.com/

sabrina@franchiseba.com

407-856-0611

Franchise Partners

Chapter

Lifestyle Is The New Wealth
Linda Ballesteros

Linda Ballesteros

Mpower Franchise Consulting

As a Certified Franchise Broker, Linda taps into her 30-plus years in the banking industry as well as her coaching background to guide and empower those who are seeking to build wealth and leave a legacy through owning a business by selecting a strong growing franchise.

Her passion is to be a catalyst to help others, through franchising, to be a business owner. She achieves this by finding the up-and-coming franchise that is best suited for your passion and skills.

She is a speaker and bestselling author, as well as a Certified Professional Life Coach, Certified Goal-Setting Coach, Certified Mindfulness Coach, and Certified Law of Attraction Coach. You can also catch Linda on the *All Things Franchising* radio show, where she interviews franchisors, franchisees, and those who support this fast-growing business model.

www.MpowerFranchiseConsulting.com

Linda@MpowerFranchiseConsulting.com

https://www.linkedin.com/in/lindaballesteros/

https://www.facebook.com/MpowerFranchiseConsulting

https://www.facebook.com/AllThingsFranchising

832-640-4922

LIFESTYLE IS THE NEW WEALTH

By Linda Ballesteros

Today more than ever, people are in transition. They are worried about paying bills, having health benefits, and supporting their family. It is during these times that we are challenged to look outside the box at what is in our best interests and make a change.

This the perfect time to ask yourself:

Does this career really make me happy?

What other profession or industry am I drawn to?

Are there business opportunities that can provide me the work-life balance I desperately seek?

If this pandemic has taught us anything, it is that we do not want to look back at life with regrets.

Maybe your corporate position requires you to be away from your family more than you would like.

When was the last time you planned and kept a "date night" with your significant other?

Do you miss your children's ball games, school programs, or dinner time discussions?

"The price of anything is the amount of life you exchange for it." ~ Henry David Thoreau

Have you ever held a position where you felt unappreciated? You do a really great job, receive bonuses and promotions, however, at the end of the day, the leadership team can be replaced. When a company goes through restructuring or is acquired by the competition, more times than not, the new CEO wants to change focus and direction or at least bring his own handpicked team into the picture. This means the position you sacrificed for can change or disappear with the stroke of a pen. With few exceptions, most companies do not offer anything that remotely resembles work-life balance, plus there is no such thing as corporate loyalty these days. This tends to cause employee performance and morale to drop, which will ultimately be felt by the customer.

I have heard from more than one of my clients that they feel they are reaching their financial peak in corporate America. In fact, some feel the only way to earn more money is to go out on their own. Executive recruiters echo this by saying that by the time employees reach their fifties, there are fewer job opportunities with acceptable compensation and benefits.

The longer you stay in a job giving 50% of your effort, the longer you put off giving 100% of your effort to creating something of your own. I know because I was in corporate banking for 30-plus years. Each year, I received raises, bonuses, and promotions; however, I was still left feeling less than fulfilled. In 2004, I left the comfort of the familiar to become an entrepreneur. Even though it has been a huge challenge and learning curve, I have never once looked back with regret.

Starting a business from the ground up can be challenging in so many ways. Not only are you perfecting your product or service, but the more daunting task is building the business infrastructure. What systems will you need to support running your business? Which accounting platform should you select? Is there an industry-specific CRM, and does it integrate with your other systems? These are just a few of the initial items, and we haven't even begun to address "marketing."

Franchising has been referred to as a "business in a box." I think this oversimplifies what you receive when you purchase a franchise; however, the idea is that you are buying into a team of experts.

Experts in the specific industry.

Experts in staffing.

Experts in human resources.

Experts in marketing.

Experts in social media.

Experts in building a successful business.

Have you ever heard the saying, "You miss 100% of the shots you don't take?"

If buying a franchise is something you genuinely want to do, you have to take that shot, or you will always wonder how your life would have been different had you had taken that step.

Taking that first step can be scary, especially if business/franchise ownership is new to you. Therefore, having a franchise broker by your side during this journey will be more valuable than you can imagine.

If you are searching for an opportunity to create a living for you and your family, or if you are seeking the vehicle that will help upgrade your lifestyle or, better yet, allow you to create a legacy, it starts with the first step. Finding the right franchise opportunity that can make your dreams come true starts with working with the right franchise broker.

There are more than 3,000 franchise opportunities out there, with another 300-plus new brands embracing the franchise model each year. Doing the research on your own could become very daunting and discouraging. In fact, your search could end before your even get started.

You see, the internet is a valuable tool for research. It has more information and statistic than you will know what to do with; howcvcr, it is limited.

Yes—it is true.

The internet is limited.

If you rely on search engines to producc rcsults, you will only find the companies that have paid to be listed high in the search rankings. High visibility on the internet does not correspond to the relative value of a business opportunity. Due to the immense amount of data that is available on the Internet, it tends to create more questions than answers, and it can be a frustrating experience.

This is where a good franchise broker can help save your dream.

Just like the best real estate brokers ask a lot of questions of their clients before touring homes, so does a good franchise broker. The more they know, the more they can present the right opportunities to the client. A franchise broker's job is to learn all they can about a franchisee candidate. What are their skills, passion, and vision for their future? Once the broker has spent time with their clients, they can present several concepts that are a good match. Most brokers will have information and knowledge about these options that are not readily accessible on the internet for the casual browser.

Like any investment, buying a franchise business carries risk. Using a franchise broker does not remove all the risk, but it can help minimize it. However, it is important for someone buying a franchise to be as diligent about choosing the broker they work with as they are about exploring franchise opportunities.

You see—all brokers are not the same.

Finding the one that best listens to you, sees your vision, and wants to help you succeed will require time before you start this journey. There will also be moments you flinch and wonder if this is the right decision. A good broker will remind you why you started this journey and not let you lose sight of your dream.

"All successful people are big dreamers. They imagine what their future could be, ideal in every respect, and then they work every day toward their distant vision, that goal or purpose." ~ Brian Tracy

I strive to build lasting relationships with my clients. I understand that this is a huge investment, and I want to be with them until they take flight. Having a background in life and business coaching, I offer my coaching services to my clients for the first three months they are in business. When you open for business, it is important to surround yourself with those who want to see you succeed and fulfill your dreams. I want to be one of those trusted advisors you choose to be on your team.

Once you have completed the search for your franchise broker and you connect with the one who is the best fit for you, the information gathering process begins.

When I work with clients, we first focus on what their lifestyle is now and what they want it to look like. You might think this is working backward; however, if the franchise you choose does not fit into your life, then it will be a struggle from the beginning.

Educating my clients is critical because it provides them with the tools to make better decisions. If they have a clearer understanding of the franchise business model and how it is different from an independent business, they can ask better questions, which is a confidence builder.

"Knowledge is life with wings." ~ William Blake

There are many advantages to getting help from a professional who knows the franchise business model, industries, and concepts. Just having someone who can help interpret the jargon can be a tremendous help.

Most people would not go to court without a lawyer or purchase a home without the help of a realtor. A franchise broker—also referred to as a franchise consultant—can help you identify businesses that are closely aligned with your skills, passions, and lifestyle goals. Yes, you could spend months researching different options on your own, but with all your efforts, you could still miss the one opportunity that is perfect for you. A competent broker can help you focus on businesses that have met certain quality standards and help you avoid making a potentially big mistake.

In the final analysis, the choice and the responsibility for researching the opportunity are yours, but as you contemplate such a huge decision, you should not leave any stones unturned. A broker is one of the best resources you can employ. Working with a good franchise broker will save you money, time and energy retrieving the right information. Using their tools and knowledge, brokers can help you weed through information. The right broker is focused on matching you with the right concept, not just selling you the franchise.

If you are not aware of what is available in the market, a franchise broker is the go-to professional.

Most brokers are compensated by the franchisor, which means their service is free to you.

If you are looking to transition out of your corporate job or maybe retired life just isn't for you right now, then I would recommend considering a franchising opportunity.

If you feel like your work-life balance needs adjusting—then, again, you might want to consider talking to a franchise broker.

Like I said earlier, there is typically no cost to you.

So, what have you got to lose?

Start now toward living the life you want to live, not the one you think you have to live.

So, the question becomes:

Why not use a broker?

Chapter

Two

But Why Not You
Carey Gille

Carey Gille

Franchise FastLane President

Carey is a serial entrepreneur, having co-founded four different start-ups throughout her career. She also brings extensive franchise experience, having franchised with two different concepts on the "zee" side while also leading franchise development for multiple brands on the "zor" side. She co-founded *ItsDeductible*, which was later acquired by Intuit and is still utilized by TurboTax users today. She then traveled the country as primary spokesperson for ItsDeductible/Intuit and was a featured guest on CNN Headline News, MSNBC, US News and World Report, Wall Street Journal, and more. Carey also co-founded Sojern, which is currently the world's largest boarding pass and travel data advertiser.

Ryan Zink and Carey worked together to award over 240 Complete Nutrition locations in less than 18 months, gaining the recognition of Entrepreneur Magazine as "Number Two Top New Franchise." Shortly thereafter, they partnered to found Franchise FastLane. FastLane is a boutique franchise sales organization partnering with over a dozen of the strongest brands in franchising to lead their franchise development and accelerate their growth nationwide. FastLane has been ranked by Entrepreneur Magazine as a top-five franchise consulting company for two consecutive years.

Carey is married, and keeps up with three active boys. She loves to read, write and run!

www.franchisefastlane.com

cgille@franchisefastlane.com

fastleads@franchisefastlane.com

www.linkedin.com/in/careygille/

www.linkedin.com/company/franchisefastlane/

www.instagram.com/franchisefastlane/

www.facebook.com/FranFastLane/

531.333.3278 (FAST)

BUT WHY NOT YOU?

By Carey Gille

As a serial entrepreneur, and a new venture adrenaline addict who also needs a clear picture of provision, VISION might be my favorite word in the entire Webster's dictionary. VISION is defined as "a clear and compelling picture of a preferable future." After an early career spent exploring the two parts of that definition as if they were separate, I am sold out to franchising as the ideal combination. It takes "a preferable future" and wraps it up in "a clear and compelling picture." Franchising gives the gift of VISION.

But I'm getting ahead of myself. We'll get to that. First, let's back up and look at that definition. "A preferable future" implies something different, something better than our present. Isn't it true that so many of us literally long for a better future? But the inability to define, articulate, or maybe even just cast a wild guess at that future holds us back.

And "a preferable future" isn't enough. You have to add to that "a clear and compelling picture." It's clear, you can see it in high-res, and yes (YES!), it is indeed better. It's what you long for! In fact, it's that very thing you think about when the meeting or the drive gets too long, and your mind wanders, explores, or even gets completely lost on its own with no guardrails.

Now bring those two parts together to have (#1) a clear and compelling picture of (#2) your preferred future, and you have VISION. What? Did you just roll your eyes? You think

VISION is only for others? You think you are just supposed to keep setting your alarm and walking through each day, year, or decade in your daily grind taking time now and then to grab a book or watch a series or listen to a podcast in which you get to escape for a minute or two, only to witness others achieve and experience VISION?

But why? Why not you?

TWO CAREER EXTREMES

The definition of VISION is so simply stated. It's short without elaborate flowery descriptors. You don't have to go look up more words to define the definition. (Ugh…frustrating.) It's simply put, but don't be fooled; it's not simply achieved. The truth is most of us don't even know where to start to achieve VISION.

Often the two parts of VISION feel like they're impossible to bring together. Indeed, throughout my career, I've experienced them as extreme ends of a spectrum. On one end, the highs of pressing toward "a preferable future," and on the other, the predictability of "a clear picture"—the rush and the stability. But in franchising, I found both. I found VISION.

I wanted to be an entrepreneur from the very beginning. I didn't want a job; I wanted a mission from the time I was very young. I graduated during the dot-com boom when everyone wanted to be in tech, so that's where I started. I was involved in a couple startups, one that began to get some early traction, primarily due to media. We didn't have a marketing budget, so we wrote press releases in the hopes of budget-friendly media exposure instead. It worked. We started getting local media exposure, so we sent a press release to the Wall Street Journal. I am twenty years past this story, and I still feel amazed and shocked every time I get to tell that they ran that release on the front page right above the fold. (Yes, as in the physical printed, black and white version of the Wall Street Journal—it used to be a thing.)

The next two years were a whirlwind. I had only filed my own taxes apart from my parents' for a few years, but overnight I was a featured tax expert and spokesperson on CNN Headline News, MSNBC, US News and World Report, and other national news outlets. We went on to sell that company to Intuit, the makers of TurboTax, and today, our tool is still part of the TurboTax experience.

I will never take for granted the opportunity to learn from, listen to, and sit across the conference table from the corporate icon, Scott Cook. It was there that I grew in my passion for service and products that are unequivocally committed to the voice of the customer, developed to exceed customer expectations and achieve high net promoter.

Those first career experiences with tech startups definitely delivered that "preferable future." Owning my own business, building my dream, impacting customers while still prioritizing my own little things. At the time, pre-kids, that was long runs, good books and the occasional girl's night. That said, I remember well wearing every single hat—marketing, legal, finance, but then the garbage had to go out too. I even remember officing out of McDonald's, because my business partner's dog broke my computer when we tried using his kitchen. I remember discussing who got a paycheck last month and who really needed one this month. Benefits, retirement (pfff)—no, those were never discussed.

When my partners and I sold that first company and landed in corporate America, I saw the benefits of the "clear picture" part of that VISION definition. There was predictable income, steady raises, defined vacation, and foreseen retirement. In my case, there was even sun every day and a very official-looking badge with my picture and title as the corporation was a high-tech, Silicon Valley, Fortune 500 company. Ah—a clear picture. It was nice! I thought I might even get used to it.

And, of course, that clear picture can be quite compelling in corporate American. You get to wear one hat, and usually one that fits you pretty well. If you are creative, you work in design or marketing. If you are analytical, maybe you're in finance. Oh, and the resources—you don't draw up a logo, hand it around the office for a quick vote, and go to print. You conduct research to tap into the voice of the customer through focus groups and in-depth interviews, carefully gathering qualitative and quantitative analytics to ensure you have the correct color, font, shape, and design to elicit just the right emotional response. That's how you do it because you can—budget and resources say you can.

Many of you are very successful in corporate America. You're challenged, fulfilled, and content, and like I said, I get it. I think that's excellent. But some of you are wired differently, and just about the time you start to think (like I did), "I could get used to this," you realize that you really can't. I was so hungry for my return to entrepreneurialism after a few years of living in the sun. A sun that I didn't see very often due to long commutes, long days full of so many internal meetings, lots of flights, so many legal reviews, and I had such a desire to hear my own voice and return to my own little things (things less my own now as a mother).

My startup days weren't over. My partners and I went on to build Sojern, Inc., which is now the world's largest boarding pass and travel data advertiser employing hundreds and generating nine figures in annual revenue.

Mine was a career of extremes. I went from one end of that spectrum to the next, and when I recovered from the whiplash and landed in the middle, I was shocked to encounter VISION right there. Right there! VISION not just for the visionary, but for anyone who wanted it and would work hard at the pursuit.

YOU GET BOTH

I have literally spent most of my career talking to displaced business executives. Hearing about families that have moved five times for the sake of the career, but really don't want to tell their graduating senior it's time to pack the boxes yet again. Talking to a mom who has been home for ten years. She's successfully managed a busy household, volunteered for the PTO, and overseen initiatives for the neighborhood association. Add a business to this skilled project management, and you have a stand-out resume, but in the absence of that, you have a talented, mature professional looking at entry-level options.

I've talked to many a business executive who stayed loyal and thought that loyalty would be returned, only to find out the most recent reorganization "re-orged" them right out the door. Who have signed the form, took the severance, and then returned to their office to pack up years of diligent efforts and expertise to make room for a younger, less experienced replacement who will decrease payroll and bring a "fresh perspective." I've connected with mature couples done raising their families. Heard how one ran the household while the other boarded planes. Years of evening FaceTime game reviews with the kids and then quick goodnights as they crawl into beds miles apart. Now they long to spend their time together, to build a legacy for their grandkids.

You know what they all need, what I needed? Simple—...VISION. They need an opportunity to see "a clear and compelling picture of a preferable future." Of course, they want the "preferable future" part, but they also need the "clear and compelling picture." After years in corporate America, years spent honing a specific skill, years with a predictable income, predictable benefits, predictable retirement, and company Christmas parties, the idea of a start-up literally shatters their risk-ometer. (Yes, it's a thing.) Tell them they need to think of a compelling business model, then figure out marketing, finance, hiring, and strategy. Now watch them turn right back around to go brush up that resume.

Do that, or introduce them to franchising. Show them a model that is already operating, financials they can review, written job descriptions, extensive training, permits secured, defined marketing strategy backed by result-based analytics. Introduce them to business owners already in the system that they can talk to in order to better understand the nature of their role, talk through their typical day, share their experience working with the franchisor. Better yet, show them how opening right within their home market could help people, how their identity will align with a service or experience that could positively impact the lives of others.

Watch them begin to understand that being a business owner doesn't have to mean they are on their own. Quite the opposite, it could mean being part of a community (a tribe) that shares learnings and supports franchisee to franchisee growth across every region of the country. Best-selling author, Seth Godin, says, "Tribes make our lives better and leading a tribe is the best life of all." Show them how they will get to plug into that tribe to build their own tribe.

Dr. Stephen Covey is a renowned author best known for *The Seven Habits of Highly Effective People*. My favorite quote across his full series of expertise is, "Leadership is communicating to people their worth and value so clearly that they see it in themselves." Show them that—their worth and value.

And I get to do that—I get to create tribes building tribes, and spend my days showing people their worth and value so that they can go on to show others their worth and value. In franchising, I get to reveal a clear picture of a better future. I get to spend my days casting VISION and watching people catch it.

FOR ME

For me, franchising is it—it's my career endgame. I know this is my endgame because I know from experience how elusive a career of VISION, balanced between the extremes of a compelling future and a clear picture, can be, and I thrive on spending my days introducing people to tangible VISION.

I didn't find my career-endgame until I was brought in to lead development for a young franchise system. Ryan Zink had spent his entire career thus far in franchising, starting as a GNC franchisee. When I met him, he was the Co-founder and President of Complete Nutrition. He had proven out the early model but needed someone to lead growth. I didn't know franchising, but I sure knew development, and I loved fitness and nutrition. They were building a solid retail model that met the needs of customers, and the timing was right as fitness/nutrition was booming, and Amazon wasn't yet on the scene. Franchising? I didn't know it, but I was anxious to learn.

We set a goal of 22 territories; we sold over 200. My husband and I bought a few ourselves, and I fell hard for franchising. Here was "a clear and compelling picture of a preferable future" for me, for the displaced executive, for the stay-at-home mom, for the mature couple seeking a legacy. Here was VISION.

FRANCHISE FASTLANE

I worked with Ryan and the team to build an impressive franchise system that was recognized by Entrepreneur Magazine as the "Number Two Top New Franchise." Ryan and his partner went on to sell Complete Nutrition to private equity in 2015. I called him a year or so later because I wanted to get back into the game. I even had a business plan to run by him, as I truly respect him as a visionary with that rare innate ability to see what isn't. I'll never forget that lunch. He listened to my early plan and then sort of just laughed and pulled out his own, even better version. We partnered and launched Franchise FastLane in January of 2017.

We make dreams come true. (I smiled when I typed that because it sounds so very corny, but we do.) First, we grow franchise brands helping dreams come true for founders. Josh Skolnick is the founder of Monster Tree. Monster Tree removes, treats, prunes trees. When we partnered with Josh, he had less than 20 franchises open. Doesn't sound like much, but it sure was. He already had a strong business model, incredible VISION, and a truly remarkable work ethic. We partnered and matched nearly 200 territories to strong franchisees, and he went on to sell Monster Tree to a consortium of leading home service brands. He did it—his VISION, his model, his plan, but what an honor to play a small part in his dream.

We also make dreams come true for franchisees. Almost every single day, we make a franchise match that creates VISION for a new franchisee. We currently represent over a dozen of the best brands in franchising—brands that smash garbage, paint houses, fix gutters, teach martial arts, deliver boutique fitness, and more.

The IFA (International Franchising Association) reports that there are over 4,000 franchise brands in the United States. Every year, approximately three hundred new brands enter, while many fail. It's is not an easy game to grow—brands struggle. FranConnect, the leading franchise CRM solution, reports that you need to talk to about 300 franchise prospects to close one good fit, and the average sales cycle to make that happen is over 200 days *(FranConnect Annual Report 2020).*

Our focus is to work closely with the right brand partners, consultant partners and qualified prospects to take all franchise growth efforts off the plate of our brands. This is important to allow them to stay focused on what they know well—their business and their commitment to supporting franchisees with robust support systems in marketing, operations, training and technology. If they do that well, franchisees can plug in, work hard, and experience VISION.

BUT WHY NOT YOU

In franchising, you don't have to wear every hat or have honed all the skills to perform every business function in order to be a business owner. The franchisor has a roadmap and strategic plan. You plug in and get to work. Note that I didn't say simply plug in. Building a business, roadmap or not, is not simple.

In franchising, you also get to make your business ownership decision armed with data. You will read a Franchise Disclosure Document that reports the details (good and bad) of the business model. Who leads and what their experience is (Item 2, Business Experience), where they might have gone wrong before (Item 3, Litigation, Item 4, Bankruptcies), what it costs to get in (Item 7, Investment), what franchisees could make (Item 19, Financial Performance Representations), even the financial strength of the franchisor (Item 21, Financial Statements). You can call the current franchisees and ask what they think. You can get a "clear picture" to make the right decision. If you're willing to work hard to choose the right model and then plug into the strategic plan, it's there right within franchising. So really, why not you? It was Henry Ford that said, "Whether you believe you can or you can't, you're right.

Premier Martial Arts was founded by industry icon Barry Van Over. He has such a passion for empowering kids through martial arts. Here again, we are so honored that FastLane gets to play a small role in his VISION. I spoke at Premier's annual symposium recently, and I was once again reminded why I love my gig. Their 100th school was opened by Scott Raven, who decided it was time for more. Here is just an excerpt from his story:

"If you asked me three years ago what I saw myself doing right as I was dealing with having been laid off for the first time, I certainly wouldn't have said franchise owner. After a grueling six-year stint, climbing the ranks in a single discipline, being laid off was cathartic. But as time wore on, a new need emerged—to build my legacy. I realized I wanted my legacy to be about the lasting impact I left on others—more relational than transactional."

In these stories, "a clear and compelling picture" and "a preferable future" meet. I love franchising from the "zor" (franchisor) side, from the "zee" (franchisee) side, and most of all, from the "dev" (development) side. Being the one who gets to grow incredible brands while giving the gift of VISION to new franchisees. That's where I sit today (or more like run, stretch, jump, leap, catch my breath—there isn't much sitting).

As I started working on this chapter, I wrestled with once again wondering if I had anything to say that would impact you, a reader with interest in business ownership. I value my career journey and what I've learned. I frankly just love what I do today and how it fulfills me and benefits others while also providing for my family. But is it truly of interest to others?

I was driving home after a long day, when a FastLane women who I highly respect called. She had some logistical questions that we resolved. Then, to my complete surprise, she said, "I won't keep you too long, but I have just one more thing." And, as if she knew I was in the middle of writing this submission, she challenged me to be more deliberate in sharing my story, even in building a brand as an experienced executive woman in the franchise industry. She explained that she had just listened to me deliver a keynote at a franchising conference, and she really felt that my passion and my experiences would interest and benefit others. Here it was again—this challenge to create VISION. She said, "Carey, why not you?"

She was right. VISION is my endgame, so why not me? And why not you?

Chapter

Three

How To Franchise Your Business
Tom DuFore

Tom DuFore

Big Sky Franchise Team

Tom DuFore is the CEO of Big Sky Franchise Team, a franchise consulting firm that helps entrepreneurs franchise their business and helps franchisors grow. Since 2003, he has consulted with thousands of companies on franchising their business and advised some of the who's-who in franchising, including Two Men and a Truck, Blimpie, Massage Envy, Ford, Matco Tools, The Total Gym, Rosati's Pizza, Medifast, Mad Science, Restoration 1, Berlitz, and many others. Tom has also led the Big Sky Franchise Team to be an award-winning and nationally recognized company. Some of the awards include Entrepreneur Magazine's Top Franchise Supplier as the number three franchise consultant, the Best Franchise Consultancy in the USA, the Top 100 Small Business award, and the 50 Most Innovative Companies to Watch.

Mr. DuFore is also a franchisee and has led his local franchise to be recognized as the number five restoration contractor in Georgia. Tom is also proud that the franchisor awarded one of his staff members "Office Professional of the Year."

To educate and better connect his clients with his extensive network, Tom hosts a weekly podcast titled, *Multiply Your Success*. Mr. DuFore holds an undergraduate degree in Management from Elmhurst University and an MBA from DePaul University.

www.BigSkyFranchiseTeam.com

Podcast:

https://podcasts.apple.com/us/podcast/multiply-your-success-with-tom-dufore/id1518562762

https://open.spotify.com/show/1QeyDYyqwRKpJw0fjWdUUA

tom@bigskyfranchise.com

https://www.linkedin.com/in/tomdufore/

Instagram:

@BigSkyFran

@TomDuFore

https:www.instagram.com/tomdufore/?hl=en

https://www.facebook.com/bigskyfranchiseteam/

855-824-4759

HOW TO FRANCHISE YOUR BUSINESS

By Tom DuFore

If you are like many successful business owners, you have thought about franchising your business at one point or another. The problem is that you probably did not know where to start, or you weren't sure if your business would be a good fit. If you run a profitable business and want to expand, you are in a great position to consider franchising. This chapter focuses on providing you, the entrepreneur and business owner, with an overview on why companies franchise, the criteria to determine if your business is franchisable, and a three-step process on how to franchise your business.

Why franchising your business makes sense

In short, franchising is a method of distribution. It allows you to replicate your business without investing your money or time to open up an additional unit. Franchising also gives you a way to grow faster than you are right now. Franchising your business provides you the opportunity to help budding entrepreneurs gain the confidence to start that business they have always dreamed about opening. There are three primary reasons why franchising your business makes sense, which include an alternative way to raise money, finding and keeping a management team, and the ability to multiply. Let us break down each one of these reasons in a little more detail.

Money

When you look to open up your next location or territory for your business, you have to come up with all the money to make it happen. To fund the expansion, you need to make it work with cashflow, take out a loan, or find investors. In each of these cases, you are giving up something substantial to expand. If you cashflow the expansion, you are likely to grow much slower, and it will cost you profit and reinvestment back into your business. If you take out a loan, *you* are 100% responsible for securing the loan, putting the collateral up, and for paying the loan back. If you take on investors, you are giving up equity in your business; plus, investors are hard to find.

The last way to raise capital to grow your business is through the use of franchising. Franchising allows you to leverage other people's money to grow your business. When a franchisee purchases a franchise, *they* become responsible for funding all expenses to open the business. The franchisee is responsible for purchasing inventory, equipment, marketing, leasehold improvements, vehicles, or any other start-up and operating expense the new territory will need.

Management

Opening a new territory or a new location for your business will require people to run and manage it. Franchising solves this critical problem of finding and keeping quality managers by securing a vested owner-operator. In most cases, the franchisee owns and operates the business. In addition to putting up the capital to launch and grow the company, the franchisee also manages and runs the business. The franchisee is responsible for finding, hiring, and retaining its staff to operate the business.

Multiply

Franchising provides you with an expansion vehicle to grow your business faster. Most business owners only ever open up one or two territories or locations. Franchising gives you the power to grow at a speed you prefer, which can range from a moderate pace to an exponential rate. One example to consider is if you only ever sold one franchise per year, you would have 20 franchises open in the next 20 years! For most business owners, this growth rate would be faster than they would have done otherwise. Franchising is a truly incredible multiplier.

When to franchise your business

The next step to franchising is to take a look at how you know if your business is ready to be franchised. In other words, are you franchisable? The following five criteria will help you assess the viability of franchising your business. Remember, this list is not exhaustive, and there are always exceptions to every rule, but it will provide you with a good starting point and understanding.

Profitable prototype

Do you have an operating business, and is it profitable? Many business owners who are asked this question will say, "Well, my tax return doesn't show that I'm profitable." This question is looking to answer if someone can fundamentally make a living running and operating your business as a franchisee. Of course, an assumption is built into that question assuming a franchisee will follow your franchise systems and work the business. Business owners take their owner's compensation in many different ways. You may take your compensation through distributions, dividends, salary, profit, employing family or friends, having a company vehicle, or other ways in which owners take income out of their business. Your franchisees will also take their owner compensation as it works best to fit their preference.

National customer base

When you begin franchising your business, it is important to make sure there is a large enough customer base. Preferably you will want to make sure there are customers for your product or service on a national basis. At a minimum, there will need to be a regional customer base, and, ideally, you will have an international customer base. The point here is when you franchise, you want to make sure there is enough room to grow. For example, you might be interested in opening 200 franchises today, but you might sell the company in the future to a new owner looking to grow the business to 2,000 franchises.

Average business model

A common misconception with franchising is that you must have "the world's greatest business model." The fact is most franchise companies have average business models. Having an average business model that is repeatable is the critical component. Don't get caught in the "it has to be perfect" trap. Your business and system will never be perfect. You will always be changing, tweaking, and fine-tuning your business model, so do not get hung up on waiting to franchise until your business is perfect.

Train and coach

When you franchise your business, you will need to teach and train your franchisees how to run all aspects of the business. The best way to think of training your franchisee is to imagine how you would prepare a general manager to run your business if you were to move hundreds of miles away. What would you do in this situation? What types of training would you put in place to ensure the general manager knew what they needed to do? Now take these thoughts and apply them to training your franchisees. When you become a franchisor, it is your responsibility to train and support your franchisees. Are you ready to be a coach? Can you teach someone how to run your business in as little time as one day to as much time as two months? One caveat is if your franchise requires special certifications or pre-requisites to becoming a franchisee. For example, a veterinarian franchise will need someone to be a veterinarian, or an engineering franchise may require someone to be a professional engineer.

Return on cash investment

The final point of discussion is the return on cash investment. It is recommended that businesses have confidence in showing a 20% return on cash investment after the second year of business and make a manager's salary. Let's break this sentence down. The 20% return on cash is the total amount of money invested into starting the franchise minus any loans taken out to run the business. For example, if someone opened up a restaurant franchise that cost $300,000 and took out a loan for $200,000, the total cash investment would be $100,000. A 20% return on cash investment in this example would be $20,000 ($100,000 x 20%) for a franchisee to see after finishing their third year in business. The manager's salary will vary widely based on the type of industry, specific company, and the location of where the business is operating. The franchisee will take the manager's salary if the franchisee is an owner-operator. If the franchisee is not an owner-operator, then the franchisee will hire a manager to run the business.

Three-Step process to franchise your business

Once you decide to franchise your business, the following is the three-step process to franchising your business. These steps are part of the Big Sky Proven Process we use at our company, and it is what we recommend you use as a roadmap in franchising your business. The process is broken down into three primary steps.

Plan

When you franchise your business, you are going to need to put together a franchise business plan. We call this your Franchise Blueprint®. This Franchise Blueprint® will need to identify and put together your expansion strategy, financial models, and competitive benchmark analysis. Some of the critical elements your franchise business plan should identify and include are the: franchise fee, royalty, marketing fees, technology fees, products sales, competitive benchmark assessment to properly assess what your franchise competition is doing, buyer profile, marketing budget, initial training, ongoing support, five-year cash flow projections for what an average franchisee would look like and a five-year cash flow projection for you as a franchisor (remember you are in a new business now).

Document

Once your plan is in place, you will need to put together the remaining documentation and collateral materials to franchise your business. The documents will include completing a franchise disclosure document (FDD), a franchise manual, a franchise marketing plan, and a franchise brochure.

Franchise Disclosure Document—The uniform franchise disclosure document, commonly referred to as the FDD, is the legal requirement to franchise your business. There are 23 points of disclosure required in the FDD, and there are several states that have additional filing or registration requirements. It is recommended that, as you go through the franchise legal process, to make sure you have engaged an experienced franchise attorney.

Franchise Manual—You will need to have your processes and systems documented as you start franchising your business. The manual will become an extension of your legal documents to define your standards and procedures. Remember, the manual is never a final product; instead, it becomes a starting point. Your franchise manual will always be evolving and updating as your business model and system grow.

Franchise Marketing Plan—The franchise marketing plan is specific to franchise lead generation and *not* to generate more customers for your business. This plan should focus on franchise recruitment efforts targeting the franchisee profile and marketing budget you identified in your previous planning.

Brochure—You will need to have a marketing response piece to provide to a prospective franchisee candidate. Once the franchise inquiry comes, you will need to have a marketing response piece such as a PDF brochure, a franchise website, or a printed brochure.

Execute

The last step of the franchising process is the one that makes your franchise company grow or not. As a franchisor, you have three jobs to execute: sell, train, and support. Selling means implementing your franchise marketing plan, generating leads, following-up with your leads, and selling franchises. Training means you need to train your franchisees on how to run your business, use your systems, and how to use your franchise manual. Supporting your franchisees means that you are regularly communicating with your franchisees, improving your systems, adding new marketing initiatives, and providing ongoing training. The execution becomes the difference between those franchise companies doing well and those franchise companies doing great.

In closing, franchising your business is a multiplier to grow faster and farther than you otherwise would without it. Franchising is a journey and is something you should not rush through. Take your time, conduct your due diligence, hire professionals and consultants to support you, and have fun! You have built your current business to success, and you can do it again as a franchise company this time.

Take a FREE franchise quiz:

https://bigskyfranchiseteam.com/franchise-questionnaire/

Chapter

Four

The Fine Art Of Avoiding Failure

Laura Canada Lewis

Laura Canada Lewis

Franchise Attorney

Law is a second career for Laura Canada Lewis, following a successful career in construction and real estate where she built and divested several companies. With first-hand experience as a business owner, and an exceptional legal education, Laura has become a well-rounded and highly desired legal advisor. Laura has walked in her client's shoes and understands their challenges, concerns, and needs as a business owner.

Laura Canada Lewis focuses her practice on serving businesses with a full spectrum of legal services to include litigation, franchising, real estate, corporate structuring, and transactions. She is nationally recognized for her legal expertise as a Franchise Legal Eagle, Super Lawyer, a Best Lawyer in Dallas, and Best Lawyer in Texas.

Laura, and her firm, provide clients with a personalized level of service often lacking in today's legal organizations. She takes the time to understand her client's aspirations, their goals, their dreams, and then crafts innovative legal solutions for every aspect of their business. Laura, and her team, are there every step of the way, facilitating negotiations, creating disclosures and contractual documentation, resolving conflicts, and serving her clients as a legal expert, trusted business advisor, and fierce protector.

www.CanadaLewis.com

LLewis@canadalewis.com

linkedin.com/in/canadalewis

www.facebook.com/canadalewislaw

469-664-0120

THE FINE ART OF AVOIDING FAILURE

By Laura Canada Lewis

After many years in the franchise industry, I have developed a healthy love-hate relationship with franchising. For franchisors, franchising is an excellent growth vehicle that allows for low-cost expansion with a better educated and more dedicated workforce. For franchisees, it is a pathway to more personal freedom and greater financial wealth through self-employment. Unfortunately, these statements are only true when both sides—franchisors and franchisees—are working together toward the mutual success of the other. Even more unfortunate for both sides is that the contracts and rules have been designed to restrain the outliers in the industry—both franchisors and franchisees—who are not committed to working hard and building successful businesses together but are more interested in the free ride they hope to get along the way.

As we all know, there are no free rides, and franchising is no different.

The vast majority of franchisors enter the industry as successful entrepreneurial operators who want to share their experience and opportunity with others. Because franchising is heavily regulated at the state and federal levels, new franchisors must learn all the nuances of the law so that they can build successful and legally compliant systems. To say the least, this is not the fun part, but it is critical to building a stable foundation for the future franchise system. In my practice, I spend a good deal of time helping new franchisors build their initial program, draft their disclosure documents, and understand how to legally sell franchises in the United States and abroad. On the other side of the coin, my firm has taken over legal representation of franchise systems where this foundation was lacking, and the franchisor and its management team were facing significant civil fines and even criminal penalties for the illegal sale of franchises because their disclosure documents were not complete and they were not properly registered in the states where they were operating or selling. This can be a terrifying event for an inexperienced management team with no idea there was any such liability associated with franchising. While my firm was able to work with state investigators and examiners to negotiate workable solutions (and no one went to jail), it was a distraction from the operations of the business and a heavy drain on financial resources that could have been avoided. Building a good legal foundation is critical.

Once the system foundation is built, the franchise system is ready to begin inviting others to buy a franchise. This is usually where the franchisor shines! Good franchisors add immediate value by sharing their experience, training, and systems so that franchisees can avoid the expenses and the learning curve of starting an independent small business. Beyond good support, buying a franchise gives you credibility with the public as a member of a regional or national brand that has longevity in the marketplace and goodwill in the hearts of local customers. This quickly takes your independent business and elevates it above other “mom and pop” shops you’ll compete with in the marketplace.

My firm has the privilege of representing several franchise brands in a wide variety of industries. Most of them were started by successful entrepreneurs who have a heart for sharing their success with others. These entrepreneurs started their franchise system to share opportunities and expertise with like-minded people who want to work hard and build their own successful businesses. These franchisors are driven by much more than royalty payments to grow their franchise systems. But since we are talking about royalties, let me take a moment to discuss royalty payments. Franchisors have large investments of time and money in their systems, support teams, legal compliance, and trademarks. They package all of this into a franchise agreement where they agree to provide these valuable assets to its franchisees on day one with an owner financing plan. The "owner financing" is royalty payments. Since the average franchisee could not afford to pay for the full value they receive under the franchise agreements at the time of signing, they are given a five- or ten-year payment plan where they pay their franchisor for these assets over time as a percentage of their gross revenue. Franchisees should also remember that royalties are the only source of revenue a franchisor receives, and this revenue source is necessary to provide marketing and operational support services that are necessary for the success of the brand.

The amount of royalty payments collected by the franchisor should be disclosed in the franchise disclosure document ("FDD"). Beyond royalties, the FDD is required to disclose all the fees you will be required to pay to the franchisor in connection with owning the franchised business. In addition to the fees you will pay and estimated start-up costs, the FDD discloses other information and risks that could be material to your decision to buy the franchise. Also included in the FDD is the form of franchise agreement you will be asked to sign if you elect to buy the franchise. Regardless of what your franchise salesperson might tell you, the terms of the franchise agreement are the terms and conditions that will govern your franchise relationship. It is very important that you understand it.

Over the years, I have received numerous calls from unhappy franchisees who invested $500K or more in a franchised business without having first investing $2500 with a franchise attorney who could educate them about the agreements they were signing or the obligations they were undertaking. I often wonder if any of these people who buy a home without hiring a home inspector and appraiser to help them ever investigate the home prior to purchasing. In my experience, oftentimes, mortgage companies require an appraisal and inspection before they lend money on a home, but that is usually not the case with small business loans. Don't let this be you! Read the documents you are given and hire an experienced franchise attorney to help you understand your rights and obligations before you make a significant financial investment in any franchise system.

Notice that I specifically recommended a *franchise* attorney. There is a reason. Franchise law and franchise agreements have been heavily litigated and have their own case law for interpreting what the provisions mean. As a result, the average attorney may not be able to fully advise you as to the practical meaning of the provisions and how they work in real life. Beyond that, a good franchise attorney is active in franchising and knows what is happening in the market.

For example, when I review an FDD and franchise agreement for a client, I point out areas where I notice the fees or terms fall outside the current industry norms or where I think there may be opportunities to negotiate certain deal points or fees with the franchisor. Over the life of the franchise agreement, these negotiated points can add significant value to the franchised business. My firm uses this time not only for renegotiating financial terms but negotiating more practical terms affecting our clients' ability to later sell the business for a good return on your investment or close without overwhelming financial liability.

Beyond negotiating deal points, there are times when a franchise lawyer will have particular insight into the system you are investigating. For example, once, by coincidence and word of mouth referrals, I came to represent several franchisees of a start-up franchise. Unfortunately, the business sounded exciting and innovative but was actually terribly expensive to build out, provided over-priced services to the public, and was impossible to manage. The problem was compounded by a management team at the franchisor level, who was not able to properly respond to troubling market conditions affecting the franchisees. They were over-optimistic and overwhelmed. I was able to quickly work with the franchisor to help get my clients out of the failing system before the avalanche of failures crippled the business. I was also able to re-direct new clients away from that brand before they made a bad investment.

Always remember that potential franchisees have the most leverage to negotiate *before* signing the franchise agreement. After the franchise agreement is signed, the dynamics shift, and the franchisor has the leverage. There is a very limited window of time for a franchisee to negotiate the best possible deal terms they can get, and that opportunity is before signing any agreements with the franchisor. My firm uses this time not only to try renegotiating financial deal terms, but more practical terms affecting our clients' ability to sell the business or close without overwhelming financial liability.

Speaking of deal terms, here are a few things in franchise agreements that every franchisee should understand. Always check the initial term and renewal periods. The initial term is the length of time you will have the right and obligation to operate the franchise under the contract—usually 5, 10, or 20 years. Once you understand the length of the initial term, confirm whether or not you have some kind of renewal rights and what are the conditions of renewal. The term and renewal are important. Confirm that you can earn a reasonable rate of return on your investment in the initial term, and then make sure the cost and conditions of renewal are reasonable and obtainable. You don't want the future of your business to hinge on the whim of someone on the future management team that you may not know. This is important because you cannot continue to operate the franchised business without an active franchise agreement. When the franchise agreement expires or is terminated for any reason, then the franchisee is forced to stop using the name and trademarks of the franchisor and is prohibited from operating a similar or competitive business due to the confidentiality provisions and covenants not to compete that are included in every franchise agreement.

Another important thing to understand is the obligation to pay royalties. Although it seems clear to the average reader that royalties are probably a percentage of gross revenue (unless your franchise agreement has some sort of monthly minimum fee). As such, it seems reasonable to think that if you have no gross revenue, then you have no royalty obligation, but that is not true. Under the franchise agreement, you are legally obligated to operate the business for the full term of the agreement regardless of profitability or other practical consideration that dictate normal business practices. When a franchisee elects to close an unprofitable franchise, they are still legally obligated to pay the franchisor the amount of lost future royalties that the franchisor would have received through the end of the term. This can be thousands of dollars in liability add onto a franchisee who probably already lost thousands of dollars before electing to close the business. Often times, franchisors will work with franchisees who have a failing business to create an action plan to either turn it around or close it without huge liabilities to the franchisor, but there is no contractual obligation that the franchisor act benevolently. For this reason, I work with my franchisee clients to address this possibility in the franchise agreement before signing to help reduce the potential royalty liability in the event of a closure.

As you can see, the small investment in a franchise lawyer for both the franchisor and the franchisee is well worth the money. This investment comes with a quick and tangible return on investment. Not only that, good franchise attorneys have a heart for small businesses but experience with much larger operations, and you can take advantage of both. Find the right attorney for you, and they will be your promoter, partner, and protector for years to come.

Chapter *Five*

My Process As A CPA Asset To Franchise Consultants And Their Franchise-Buying Candidates

Michael Reeder, CPA

Michael Reeder, CPA

Swartz & Reeder Advisors

I am a CPA passionate about helping people buy businesses, with franchise businesses being a major component of my niche as a Business Buyer Helper.

Now I am the owner of the CPA firm that hired me out of college. It was Swartz Financial Management, Inc. then—it's Swartz & Reeder Advisors now. Grateful for my mentor and second father, Barry Swartz, CPA.

I've always had entrepreneurship in my blood. As a kid, I was passionate about running lemonade stands, selling popcorn for the boy scouts, and building haunted houses with my friends in my garage and charging for admission. This entrepreneurial spirit would manifest itself later on in life, and it did just that in 2014 and 2015.

Still Swartz Financial Management, Inc. at the time in 2014, we acquired another small CPA firm in the greater Chicago area and merged it into our main book of business. In January 2015, I became a partner, and we switched the name of the practice to Swartz & Reeder Advisors. In the summer of 2015, we purchased a second small CPA firm and merged it into our main book of business.

One of the clients retained from one of the books of business purchased was a self-employed franchise consultant. I'd never heard of a "franchise consultant" up until this point, and I asked him about his craft. He said he helps people buy franchise businesses. I thought that was pretty cool. I just bought a couple businesses myself, albeit not franchise businesses, and here I just retained a client who's in the business of helping people buy businesses. This got me excited. That entrepreneurial spirit started rising above the surface again.

E: michaelreeder@swartzreeder.com

W: www.swartzreeder.com

P: 847-241-5800 ext 2

M: 847-302-3397

MY PROCESS AS A CPA ASSET TO FRANCHISE CONSULTANTS AND THEIR FRANCHISE-BUYING CANDIDATES

By Michael Reeder, CPA

In 2015 the lightbulb turned on in my head. I decided to open my own business brokerage/franchise consulting firm from scratch and operate it as a second business simultaneously with my CPA firm. So, I did just that. But I needed someone to run the darn thing. In comes my best friend from childhood, Jon Pace, and my wife, Mimi Reeder. We haven't looked back since the birth of BizFranHub.

Upon the inception of BizFranHub, we joined the Franchise Brokers Association as broker members and attended the FBA conference in Orlando in November 2015. After a few days of networking, I quickly became known by the other brokers at the conference as "Mike, the new broker who is also a CPA." Several brokers would ask me tax/entity structure/accounting-related questions as they pertained to buyers they were currently working with. I answered question after question and realized the value I was providing.

I continued answering questions via email over the months following the conference, and met up with Sabrina Wall, CEO of the FBA, in Milwaukee, Wisconsin, in January 2016. She was in town on business checking in on a franchisor client. I was two hours south in Chicago. I drove up and met her for dinner. I left that dinner as the affiliate CPA of the FBA.

Ever since, and to this day, I've been providing a free, simple process to FBA brokers across the country. And more recently, sharing my process with members of IFPG, FCC, The You Network, FranChoice, FranNet and FranServe, along with nonfranchise business brokers affiliated with Murphy's, Sun Acquisitions, Transworld and several independents.

Since day one, my process has been this—providing free 60-minute consultation calls to buyer candidates working with my broker/consultant affiliates. I answer questions the buyers have in the context of accounting, tax entity structure funding, financial projections, resale financial statements, due diligence and franchise disclosure document (FDD) Items 19 and 21 as it pertains to their franchise investigation and investment process (also FDD Items 5,6 and 7 when requested).

I'm notorious for going over the one-hour mark if the conversation requires it. I'm notorious for scheduling free follow-up calls if the buyers want more. Yes, I provide a lot of free advice. Yes, I provide maximum value. Yes, several of these buyers circle back with me after their business purchase and work with my CPA firm in a paid context as their business CPA.

Accounting

Common topics discussed on the free consultation calls include:

Implementation of a bookkeeping system, often QuickBooks Online.

Tracking business expenses paid via personal funds and cash and recording on the books via journal entry.

Recording the Rollover as a Business Start-Up (ROBS) capitalization on the books.

Payroll journal entries.

Automation—syncing the business bank and credit card accounts to the QuickBooks.

Bank and credit card reconciliations, bill pay, invoicing, inventory tracking, payroll.

Discussing who should be the day-to-day bookkeeper and who should be the reviewer of the books, and why.

Tax

Common topics discussed on the free consultation calls include:

Income tax (federal and state).

Social security and Medicare tax (aka self-employment tax, FICA taxes).

Other payroll taxes.

Sales tax.

Flow-through taxation vs. C-Corp taxation.

Double taxation.

Understanding how income taxes are different for self-employed individuals compared to employed individuals. The internal revenue code favors the former over the latter.

Income tax mitigation strategies.

Entity Structure

Common topics discussed on the free consultation calls include:

S-Corp.

C-Corp.

LLC.

Partnership.

Sole Proprietorship.

Diving deep into the pros and cons of each type of entity structure.

Funding

Common topics discussed on the free consultation calls include:

SBA Loans.

ROBS Program (making sure the candidate fully understands this complex structure).

Other conventional business loans.

State-and-local-sponsored business loans.

401k loans (lesser of $50,000 or 50% of plan assets).

Leveraging equity in assets on personal financial statement.

Cash.

Credit cards.

Michael and Swartz & Reeder Advisors are not lenders, but we discuss funding strategy with candidates—exploring all options worth considering based on the candidate's unique set of facts and circumstances.

Financial Projections

Common topics discussed on the free consultation calls include:

For the candidate's own internal purposes:

When am I going to hit break-even?

When am I going to hit my replacement income?

When am I going to hit a profit percentage of X? Y? Z?

What will be needed if a business plan is required as part of a loan application?

A great exercise for any person planning to buy a business, if you are going into business for yourself, is to take the lead on creating your own business plan, including the financial projections section of the business plan (this is my opinion).

Resale Financial Statement Due Diligence

Common topics discussed on the free consultation calls include:

Disclaimer: I am not a Certified Business Appraiser/ Certified Valuation Analyst.

Disclaimer: I do not audit the financial statements of the seller.

Disclaimer: I do not produce a quality of earnings report or something similar to a broker's opinion of value.

I do advise buyers during the free consultation calls with strategies they can implement as part of their due diligence when negotiating with the seller on a franchise resale.

How to arrive at the seller's discretionary earnings (SDE)

Types of questions to ask the seller as part of the due diligence.

There are buyers who do retain me at my hourly rate beyond the free consultation call(s) to do my own analysis of SDE and a list of due diligence questions to present to the seller. These engagements typically require two to three hours of my time, and it's always over-communicated to the buyer that I'm not negotiating directly with the seller on behalf of the buyer, but instead providing the buyer with information to aid them in the negotiation process, and at any time the buyer is at risk of losing out to another buyer.

Item 19

Common topics discussed on the free consultation calls include:

Walking the candidate through the financial statistics found in this section of the FDD and what they mean.

A great source for data that can be inputted into the candidate's financial projections (e.g., revenue assumptions, variable cost assumptions).

Item 21

Common topics discussed on the free consultation calls include:

Walking the candidate through the franchisor's audited financial statements found in this section of the FDD and what they mean (balance sheet, income statement, statement of cash flows, statement of changes in owners' equity).

Walking the candidate through the footnotes that follow the audited financial statements and what they mean.

There are candidates who do retain me at my hourly rate beyond the free consultation call(s) to do my own analysis of the franchisor's Item 21 and list of due diligence questions to present to the franchisor. These engagements typically require two to three hours of my time

Case Study 1: Income Tax Optimization Via Entity Structure Strategy.

I had a free consultation call with a buyer. Coming into the call, he was planning on using the ROBS C-Corp structure to invest in two hair salon franchise territories. This buyer's plan was to keep his corporate job and invest in this business as a semi-absentee model. During the call, I devised a strategy of going S-Corp for the first territory and C-Corp Robs for the second territory. By doing this, the buyer was able to take his loss from the build-out and start-up phase of the first territory and flow it through to his individual income tax return, where it netted against his corporate W2 income, thus saving him thousands of dollars in taxes on his individual income tax return.

Case Study 2: More Than Just A CPA, A Business Coach Too.

A lot of the time, I serve as a coach on these calls, coming at it from the angle of a CPA. I'm a business owner, so I help buyers get in the right mindset business owners. Several times buyers are overthinking their financial projections. They feel anxiety over them. I pull them back, help them simplify the process of putting financial projections together and where to obtain information.

Owning a business isn't easy. But following the franchisor's playbook is simple. Stick to the franchisor's playbook and execute. That's a core benefit of franchise business ownership compared to independent business ownership. You are in business for yourself but not by yourself. Several buyers are nervous on the consultation calls—they are close to pulling the trigger on buying a business. And that's a big deal. It's natural to be nervous and anxious; it's expected.

I help buyers recognize all this and mentally prepare for franchise business ownership. I focus more on mentally preparing the buyers for franchise business ownership and giving free advice on things they can do themselves as opposed to trying to get them to pay me for doing a bunch of stuff. I want buyers to succeed. I do work with several buyers in a paid context down the road after the free consultation call(s), but the amount of value and advice I provide on the free consultation calls is immense, and it gives me great satisfaction to do my part to give buyers the best shot at success as franchise business owners.

The buyers appreciate my candor, straight talk and insistence on them doing several things themselves instead of paying me to do everything for them. These buyers plan to be in business for the long-term. And, so do I. I'm focused more on the long-term relationship than the short-term buck.

My process has been working thus far. As the saying goes, if it ain't broke, don't fix it.

Chapter

Six

The Franchise Model: The Perfect Epitome Of Brand Power

Suzanne Tulien

Suzanne Tulien

Brand Ascension

Brand Clarity Expert, Author, and International Speaker Suzanne Tulien is an authority in identifying and defining a business' internal Brand DNA blueprint, creating authentic positioning, and building competitive advantage by aligning leadership and employees to "out-behave" their competition, consistently.

Suzanne facilitates engaging brand strategy using her turnkey Brand DNA methodology in live events, webinars, workshops, and consulting. As the pioneer of *Ignite Your Personal Brand Presence* coaching mastermind and online course program, she is helping solo-professionals and emerging leaders own and leverage their expertise, personality, and authenticity to live their full potential. She guides businesses to get more conscious, strategic and deliberate in delivering on their brand promise and value position. She is the author of three books, *The 6 Myths of Small Business Branding*, *Brand DNA*, and her newest book, *Personal Brand Clarity; Identify, Define, and Align to Become What You Want to Be Known For*. Suzanne also trains speaker-brands to deliver their expertise to audiences that enlists, equips, and engages them to want more!

Suzanne is the founder of Brand Ascension, has over 30 years of business brand consulting experience, and is an international speaker, consultant, award-winning graphic designer, and certified trainer.

www.BrandAscension.com

www.PersonalBrandPresence.com

www.Linked.In.com/brandascension

www.instagram.com/brandascensionconsulting

Inquiry@BrandAscension.com

719.660.2533

THE FRANCHISE MODEL: THE PERFECT EPITOME OF BRAND POWER

By Suzanne Tulien

Then I had an idea. Let's invite the current owner-operators to join us (headquarters) in the process of flushing out the brand's DNA. They have a vested interest, they want to grow their businesses, they needed something to truly "hang their hats" on that they could bring back to their stores and inspire their own teams with a powerful brand construct, delivery and promise.

So, we did. And it worked. It worked so well this franchisor got the attention of a large corporation that had several national franchises under their brand and was curious about acquiring this one. And they did. My client signed the acquisition papers (willingly and excitedly) from this larger firm to help continue to scale the brand faster with much bigger operational systems and budgets!

So, I want to share with you the power of the brand within your franchise. The power of conscious, strategic, and deliberate brand clarity on a value position that truly differentiates. The power of brand consistency in building trust, history, traditions, and rituals. The coherence brand can bring to your culture. And the power of "on-brand" actions and behaviors that continue to perpetuate what you promise to deliver. Knowing your brand as a franchisee and, most importantly, a franchisor is the most powerful propagator of sustainable business growth.

First of all, every business has a brand. Whether they have formally identified and defined it or not—good, bad, or indifferent. So, it is important to establish a basic understanding of what a brand actually is. As it is often mistaken as the visual representation of trademark, trade-dress, or "logo," as most would refer to it, but to be clear—your brand is *not* your logo (graphic symbol itself), but rather the *value proposition* your logo comes to represent.

So, the question becomes, "What does your logo actually represent?" What values, personality, differentiators, standards of performance and promise does it stand for? And how are all those attributes made tangible in the delivery of your products and services, consistently? *That* is your brand!

A brand, your franchise brand, is just a perception (or set of perceptions). That's it. It lives within the minds of your stakeholders and is experienced through your actions, behaviors, services, and products.

And every business inadvertently develops a brand the moment they start doing business, whether they've identified and defined it or not. Because up to eleven perceptions are built within the first seven seconds of contact within the minds of your prospects, customers, and employees, and it doesn't stop there. If you have not yet defined and aligned to the perceptions you want others to have of you, then you are willingly enabling your prospects to be *in control* of your brand.

You can think of the process of branding as the process of assigning meaning to your value position. It is a process of assigning those specific perceptions you want others (customers, employees, community, vendors, etc.) to have of you—authentically, of course. This internally generated output is the "secret sauce" to the ability to deliver on a promise consistently, building trust and sustaining growth.

The word branding is also regularly used interchangeably with the term marketing, which is also a gross misuse, because they are two separate yet complementary functions. Let me explain as briefly as I can. You see, you market (verb) a brand (noun). And if you are marketing a brand you have not yet identified and defined, what are you actually marketing? The function of marketing is a focus on communicating and disseminating information about the brand. Branding, as I mentioned above, is about identifying and defining or assigning meaning (value position) to an entity to create distinction in the market/industry—and take to market.

When you consciously and strategically identify, define and align to your brand, you actually have more concrete promises to market (communicate) and deliver on, resulting in building a customer experience of "I got what I paid for and more,!" as well as establishing an on-brand culture of brand ambassadors who have purpose and passion for the value position.

That is the power of *brand*—when you know how to clearly define, align and leverage it.

With the space I have left in this chapter, I want to walk you through the development of a brand's DNA so that you can make it tangible in ways that carve out distinction in any competitive marketplace.

"Your marketing might get prospects in the door, but it is YOUR BRAND that keeps them coming back [and telling their friends!" ~ Suzanne Tulien

Your brand lives inside your franchise DNA. It is the core essence of its value position that should be replicable. It is exemplified by the employees, leadership, systems and processes, communications, and actions and behaviors. It is simply a matter of identifying, defining and aligning to bring it about very consciously, strategically and deliberately. So, let's get started.

Here's the dilemma. When it comes to growth, many businesses spend most of their time and budgets focused on external marketing/advertising efforts (telling customers how good they are or their product is) rather than on strategic, internal branding efforts (those efforts that help you and your teams walk your talk and to keep the customers coming back and telling their friends.) The "missing piece" of business success.

So, one question for each of the two types of readers—franchisors and franchisees:

1. How does the franchisor begin the internal brand-defining process (preferably before selling franchises to prospects—but can be done afterward with care)?
2. How does the franchisee (owner/operator) hone in on leveraging the franchisor's established brand? (Because the brand is what you invested in and is the value position you cannot let go of.)

To answer the first question in a nutshell (as this process is spelled out in my book, *Brand DNA; Uncover Your Organizations Genetic Code for Competitive Advantage*):

Identify and define your top four core *values*, preferably by engaging your current team to recognize and acknowledge what you truly care about as an organization. Don't skip over the defining of the value terms, as this is one of the most important, clarifying processes you can take to get everyone on the same page.

Identify and define your overall brand *style* within four adjectives. Your "style" is the collective personality trait of the company and how you go about delivering your products and services.

Establish key standards of performance that reflect your values and style attributes, then map out supportive actions needed to live up to those standards every quarter. These standards should be composed around the four key areas of any business: financial, customers, employees, and systems and processes.

Brainstorm your authentic *differentiators* (those quantitative differences that your competitors cannot claim) and market them, and train your people to leverage them.

Craft an inspirational, employee-focused, *brand mantra* to capture the essence of the brand's DNA and provide your employees with a highly motivational, action-oriented, easy to remember tool that keeps the brand top of mind.

Compose a purposeful Brand Promise® that cites what the brand commits to deliver day in and day out to all stakeholders.

Most importantly, infuse (align) those attributes you flush out into every facet of your business! From your customer-facing processes to your operations, human relations, and communications so that you enable and automate living your brand promise. This is how you make your brand tangible and what builds advocacy and sustains your growth!

It is time to take a step back and ask, "Are we fully walking our talk consistently?" "Do we really know who we are compared to our competitors?" "What exactly are our quantifiable differentiators?" "Are we the leader in our industry?" "Do we have high employee retention rates?" "Do we have the necessary systems and processes in place to enable us to walk the talk and deliver on our promise every—single—time?"

For the Franchisee owner/operator (question 2 from above):

When considering your investment to purchase your franchise, make sure you ask about what they believe is the brand's unique value position. Do they have a brand manual outlining the details of the core values, differentiators, promise, vision, mission, and how they've infused it into their process design to ensure it is part of the culture?

How do they hire and manage employees and inculcate them into the brand story and culture of the company?

How do they recognize and reward their employees?

What are their values on the environment, the communities they serve, and philanthropy?

How do they deal with unsatisfied clients, and how do this protocol and others tie back into the brand standards of performance?

Do they have a formal graphic standards manual that details all the key consistent visuals that represent the brand; logo/fonts/colors, interior and exterior signage, vehicle wraps, uniforms, collateral materials, forms, business cards, stationery, and so on?

What is the recommended marketing plan, and what type of support will you be receiving?

These questions will help you determine the maturity of the franchise operations you are considering owning. If you already own it, then review these questions with your franchisor if you have not yet received answers or materials to support you in perpetuating the consistency of the brand's value position within your local area.

As you can see, most of the function of successful branding starts internally from the inside out. When your Brand DNA is clearly understood, your job is to make it as tangible as possible in the minds of your audience, i.e., employees, customers, vendors, community. This is the recipe for success!

Chapter

Seven

Get Out Of Your Customer's Inbox!

Linda Ballesteros

Linda Ballesteros

Mailbox Power

As a Certified Franchise Broker, Linda taps into her 30-plus years in the banking industry as well as her coaching background to guide and empower those who are seeking to build wealth and leave a legacy through owning a business by selecting a strong growing franchise.

Linda writes in her book, *Your Pot of Gold is a Handshake Away*, that building relationships is like "magic dust" to your business growth and success. That is why she shares Mailbox Power with all of her clients as they begin building their business.

She is a speaker and bestselling author as well as a Certified Professional Life Coach, Certified Goal Setting Coach, Certified Mindfulness Coach and Certified Law of Attraction Coach. You can also catch Linda on the *All Things Franchising* radio show, where she interviews franchisors, franchisees, and those who support this fast-growing business model.

https://mailboxpower.biz/ballesteros

www.MpowerFranchiseConsulting.com

Linda@MpowerFranchiseConsulting.com

https://www.linkedin.com/in/lindaballesteros/

https://www.facebook.com/MpowerFranchiseConsulting

https://www.facebook.com/AllThingsFranchising

832-640-4922

GET OUT OF YOUR CUSTOMERS INBOX!

By Linda Ballesteros

How many emails did you have waiting for you this morning in your inbox?

Now—how many did you delete without even opening them?

Consumers are inundated with emails.

Between newsletter subscriptions, shopping receipts, delivery updates, billing notifications, appointment reminders, and marketing messages, consumers receive many more emails than they can read.

An email inbox is full of competition for the consumer's attention, making it that much harder for businesses to get noticed by their customers and prospects.

It wasn't always like this. Email has changed, and so has the consumer relationship with their inbox.

With the growth of email, the search is on for the best means to get in front of your prospect or clients. Even though there is a huge surge for brands to have a presence on every social media platform, maybe it is time to take a step back to see where you would have less competition.

Direct mail!

Statistics show some marketers see direct mail as less than effective; however, that is far from true, and the power of direct mail is underrated.

Here are some stats that may surprise you:

70% of Americans say snail mail is more personal than an email.

56% of Americans say receiving mail is a real pleasure.

39% of customers try a business for the first time because of direct mail advertising.

Over 60% of direct mail recipients were influenced to visit a promoted website.

70% to 80% of consumers say they open most of their mail, including what they label "junk."

Millennials and Generation Z are two of the most digital-savvy generations today. Studies indicate that Millennials still prefer receiving direct mail.

92% of Millennials have been influenced to make a purchasing decision by direct mail.

69% of Millennials somewhat or very much like mailed coupons for local restaurants.

75% of Millennials said that receiving personal mail makes them feel special.

62% of Millennials said they had visited a store in the past month based on information received in the mail.

When asked, "Which is more effective at getting you to take action?" 30% of Millennials said direct mail, while 24% said email.

Direct mail campaigns can be created for more than discount coupons to your local restaurant.

Would you like to close more prospects?

Sending a thoughtful and personalized gift of appreciation can help break through the inbox barrier and let your prospect know how much you would appreciate their business.

How would you like to discover the secret to staying at the top of your existing customers' minds?

Customers respond with loyalty when they receive a special gift, which shows how grateful you are that they have chosen to do business with you.

Are you looking for ways to retain good employees?

Recognizing a job well done goes a long way to create loyal employees who feel acknowledged and appreciated.

You may be thinking that this sounds like a complicated and time-consuming task that only the best direct mail marketing team could execute.

Well—that is no longer true.

I was introduced to the direct mailing service Mailbox Power, where I discovered just how easy it is to manage a campaign from my desktop computer.

It has never been easier to create custom greeting cards, send a sweet treat or a special gift with the receiver's name printed on it.

How easy would it be to design a special birthday card for a new client and schedule it to go out a few days before the actual date? This will let your clients know you care; however, it is also the perfect retention strategy. You may think, "once a client—always a client". This is no longer true! There have been thousands of dollars in business losses to the competition simply because they were not the first person to come to mind.

Let me share a story with you.

A highly successful realtor decided to reach out to past clients. To his surprise, a significant number of cards were returned, indicating the resident had moved. This sent him reeling because he had sold them the house; however, they decided to list the house and potentially purchase a new home using another realtor.

He was so certain that past clients were a "shoe-in" for future business that he failed to continue nurturing those connections.

Do you think he was financially impacted?

You betcha!

After some research, his conservative estimate was that he missed out on hundreds of thousands of dollars in commissions.

I must admit I had a similar experience as the homeowner. My late husband and I purchased a lovely home in the perfect location. We enjoyed it for more than eight years until it was clear that it had become way too much to care for, and we sought to downsize. When we talked about listing the house, and the name of our previous realtor came up, I said, "I haven't heard from him, so I am not sure he is still an agent. Why don't we call the person who has listed the house down the street?"

"Assumptions are the termites of relationships." ~ Henry Winkler

Just think about it. If that realtor has sent a holiday card or birthday card, he would have gotten the listing. By the way, our house sold in 24 hours.

Do you have clients that you have not reached out to, but want a passive, less intrusive approach over a phone call?

Mailbox Power has created a user-friendly platform that will allow you to stay in touch with prospective franchisees to help remind them of their dream to own their own business. As a franchisee, Mailbox Power will give you the tools to stay in front of your clients for future business.

"If you make a sale, you make a living. If you make an investment of time and good service in a customer, you can make a fortune." ~ John Rohn

Another feature of Mailbox Power is list building, which allows you to target a specific demographic within certain zip codes for your direct marketing campaign. Creating a postcard drip campaign is simple when you have the right tools.

So, if you are looking for a new, more effective approach to strengthening relationships with future or existing clients or if you are looking for a list building tool—Mailbox Power is the answer.

Franchisors

Chapter

Eight

Fundraising U
Mike Bahun

Mike Bahun

Fundraising University

My name is Mike Bahun. I'm a life-long coach and athlete. And I am the proud President and Founder of Fundraising University. I was a three-sport athlete of the year at Omaha Bryan High school and a Converse High School All American in baseball. I received a Division One wrestling offer from Clemson University, and was a Metro Wrestling and District Champion who broke the Nebraska state record for takedowns. I played football and received several NAIA offers, and earned 11 high school letters. At Iowa State

University, I was an All-Big 8 Outfielder and played professionally for the Sioux City Explorers. I earned a bachelor's degree from Iowa State and an MBA from Bellevue University. I went on to coach high school baseball at Omaha Bryan and Iowa Western Community College.

I am a certified trainer for Ownership Mindset and have completed a doctorate level course for the Wealth Factory on entrepreneurship and finance. I was inducted into the Omaha Metro Hall of Fame and recognized for career accomplishments athletically and professionally. In addition to Fundraising University, I'm also currently the Director of Player Development for baseball at Creighton University.

https://fundraisingu.net/franchising

mbahun@fundraisingu.net

402-680-5029

FUNDRAISING U

By Mike Bahun

Participation in high school sports is at an all-time high—but funding can't keep up. Budgets for many school districts are continuing to shrink.

Some of the first places typically cut are athletic programs, putting increased pressure on teams to fundraise. Parents also can't afford the rising cost of sports. Youth sports in the U.S. are diverging according to income—more middle and lower-income students are quitting athletics because their families can't afford it. Not only are athletics important to the students, but often sports are what I believe keep the best teachers in schools. Without sports, it would dilute the quality of teachers. The ability to lead and work with kids in a team atmosphere and the opportunities, the experiences, the relationships that are built outside of the classroom in sports are very unique.

From early on, sports and coaches inspired me. Because I grew up in a single parent, inner-city household, I sought male leadership, structure and a competitive outlet. Even from those early days, Fundraising University was beginning to take shape in my mind. As a three-sport athlete and coach at all levels from the age of eight to being a current Division One coach and a former pro athlete, I knew and believed that coaches are the heroes of our communities.

The mission of Fundraising U is best defined by this story: I was heading home after a late night conducting a football fundraiser in Atlanta. While walking to my car, I was startled when approached by an emotional mother. This single mother shared that her son, Anthony, sold his goal within the fundraiser and earned enough money so they could have him participate in football due to his school district's "pay-to-play" model. Since the family could not normally pay this fee, the fundraiser funded it solely and provided a helmet, pads, and practice gear. Anthony would now have structure, male leadership, friends, and be occupied long enough so that his mom can also work a part-time job after school and help the family. This interaction is exactly what I dreamt the company would accomplish. Our mission continues to be equipping students, coaches, and communities to dream big and raise more.

Athletic programs aren't cheap to run or participate in, and all too often, the financial burden keeps athletes from taking part. The typical family with kids who play sports spends about $700 a year on fees, equipment, and more, but some spend up to $35,000. More public schools are also charging pay-to-play fees, pricing out some families. We put a stop to that by helping high school sports programs generate the funds needed to pay for uniforms, travel, equipment, and more. Without the stress of funding, students and parents can focus more on practices, honing their skills, and chasing their dreams. For many students, athletics is their primary path to college or the driving force behind their motivation. Financial hardships don't need to be the reason for their success or failure, especially since high school participation has reached an astounding number of 7,980,886 athletes nationwide.

High school sports positively impact students in many ways, including improved academics, positive mentors, and developing leadership skills. Fundraising University is here to help you see your students achieve their dreams. Whether it's new equipment or the cost of bussing to that state championship, we make sure your team has everything they need to make it. A few extra hundred or even a few thousand dollars in the bank can help in numerous ways.

This passion for coaches and helping teams, combined with a high level of funding in schools for the survival of sports, is what founded Fundraising University! We are a professional team of former athletes and coaches that enter into schools, clubs, and academies, and contribute to the funding needed to help groups and teams. We solve this problem with a one-week fundraiser that, on average, raises $200 in profit per participant. Our vision is to unify teams, fuel programs, and to most importantly, create lasting, positive change for communities.

We live in a world of smartphones and social media, yet many fundraising programs are still stuck in the stone age. With Fundraising U, we help your team with cutting-edge fundraising tools designed to generate more funds in less time. We've stopped trying to motivate players with outdated systems, and we make it easy, enjoyable and fun for athletes. We lead with our proven sales formula that matches the right group with the right product during the right season to achieve maximum fundraising results. We work with franchisees to plan, execute, and repeat successful fundraisers with their coaches & students year after year. From the initial planning meeting through product delivery, franchise owners will be there to direct coaches and students every step of the way. Again, we do it to see kids succeed and give them opportunities, which was my dream from the very beginning of founding this company. We've organized a system that safely allows kids to ask for help and raise big for their team or program. And it's not just for sports in high schools. We will help nearly anyone who wants to fundraise, including small colleges, elementary schools, music programs, club teams, and middle schools.

We've perfected our system over the past few years to give you a streamlined fundraising program that is guaranteed to raise more money in less time. No more praying and hoping you can afford new equipment or go to that out of state tournament. With Fundraising U, we'll get you to your goal.

We plan, execute and repeat. Step by step, we plan a no-fail fundraiser and pick the perfect product to match your team's goals. Our dedicated fundraising coaches help your teams build fundraising plans and unique fundraising platforms, and train athletes to be confident fundraising machines. Between our proven formula and our wide variety of products and services to sell, our athletes will raise more than ever before. Our athletes will also have access to products that people want to buy. The fundraising coach will break the plan down into actionable goals and help players stay motivated. Time tested products like gourmet cookie dough, and seasonal treats are still relevant. But we've also found a unique and exclusive process we run with teams called FundU Now—raising money through text and phone in as little as an hour!

Step Two is executing. When your fundraising plan is solid and starts with clear expectations and incentives that are achievable and tangible for your students, they want to work for their fundraising. It puts the fun back into the process. Fundraising University provides the tools and the resources to keep your students motivated and target goals to hit and exceed. Beginning the fundraiser strongly helps your athletes stay focused on the end goal and blitz to the finish line, helping their dreams become a reality. Fundraising University coaches deliver the prizes and purchased products to coaches and students and teach them about the power of motivation and succeeding at their goals. During the fundraising process, students learn valuable life skills that will help them in their futures, beyond school and sports.

And our final step is to repeat! With the success of a fundraiser, the coach will never need to pursue another fundraising program, because our formula takes into consideration the needs of the customers. We work tirelessly to maintain products that people want to buy. We work for coaches, students, and their parents to create a fundraising experience that brings customers back ready to support athletics programs even after students graduate. We pride ourselves on building relationships, and 88% of our teams work with us again!

We have raised over $125 million for teams and groups in 11 years, and to propel our growth, we initiated a franchise model to continue our mission. Launched in 2009, we are now an industry leader servicing eight states. Why Fund U? It's a home-based business with zero to one employees to start. Other benefits: low start-up, low overhead, up and running in 60-90 days, and we offer extensive training, full marketing support, and robust technology systems. Not to mention a proven simple sales system that drives recurring revenue and strong returns. As a franchisee, you can expect outstanding support across all areas, including operational support, marketing, purchasing support, accounting, legal, and research and development.

We supply extensive training to get you up and running like a pro! We provide a 45-day training program complete with a selling certificate, our unique service-based approach mastered, operations training, business management, and goal setting with over 96 years of combined industry experience. This 45-day training is just the start and continues with weekly, monthly, quarterly, and a biannual system with two, four-day, in-person meetings each year. We have over ten years with over eight locations in our Item 19 and a very low Item 7, and franchises can easily achieve over a 20% EBITA.

Training topics will include administration, operations, sales/marketing, and on-the-job training. We also offer step-by-step sales cycle training, lead generation, and funnel management. On-site training will be held at the franchisee's location for three to five days to assist in the commencement of operations. During this time, an experienced trainer will make sales calls right alongside new reps and then continues to coach the rep on securing leads and building the sales funnel. Tech Tool Training Technology will also be a focus of training to ensure proficiency across our standard technology, including CRM, Google Suites, Asana and Fan Club.

Our business is transformational, and you have to appreciate the interaction and what you're contributing to—students, teachers and schools. Our journey as a franchisee is one that requires many skills and has an 86% success rate of earning six figures after three years of dedication. I believe these skills are being competitive, organized, teachable, and empathetic. A consistent demonstration of these skills, coupled with an 88% residual rate with customers, will create the essence of a win-win-win!

I'm proud to share that we are also a company that makes a difference in the community in many ways, including The Coaching Matters Foundation. Coaching Matters is a nonprofit foundation built to help coaches succeed. As I've mentioned, coaches can be one of the most influential people in a child's life. Coaches serve as teachers, guides, mentors, and friends. But coaches need support, too. Coaching Matters Foundation, LLC provides consulting services regarding all aspects of the business operation. Through the associations we sponsor, we provide funds for coach training, motivational award programs, and student scholarships. We also sponsor coach and athlete recognition. By using Fundraising University, schools and teams support Coaching Matters with zero effort. A portion of every fundraiser goes toward the foundation, and therefore, back to your community. This essentially means you're giving back to the community in several ways, through the fundraiser and the foundation.

If you're ready to make a difference, we are looking for franchisees with experience in sales, networking, and customer service, as well as high personal standards and a passion for students and athletics. If you're a self-starter, competitive, ready to impact lives and consider yourself a team player, Fundraising University may be a great fit for you.

You can contact me at mbahun@fundraisingu.net or 402-680-5029. More information on Franchising in Fundraising U is also available at https://fundraisingu.net/franchising/.

Chapter *Nine*

It's A Win-Win With Clothes Bin

Nick Boariu

Nick Boariu

Clothes Bin

Nick Boariu's executive career includes over 15 years of hands-on management experience as co-founder of three national franchise brands. He is a Certified Franchise Executive (CFE) by the International Franchise Association (IFA).

Clothes Bin® Franchise ranked #391 in the 2020 Inc. Magazine's *5000 Fastest-Growing Private Companies in*

America, breaking into the elite top 500 and ranked number two in their category as a franchisor.

Mr. Boariu is a graduate of the College of Business at Florida State University, a graduate of the Jim Moran Institute for Global Entrepreneurship Executive Program, and the Winner of Florida State University's 2020 *Seminole 100 Award* for the highest compound annual growth rate (CAGR) of 100 alumni-owned businesses. Clothes Bin was recently listed in the Entrepreneur Magazine 42nd annual 2021 Franchise 500 ranking.

Nick@ClothesBinFranchise.com

ClothesBinFranchise.com

LinkedIn.com/in/Boariu
844.FLL.BINS (844.355.2467)

IT'S A WIN-WIN WITH CLOTHES BIN

By Nick Boariu

"Did you know that 85% of textiles end up in local landfills?" said Marc Douglas, co-founder of Clothes Bin® Franchise. I did not! These discarded textiles equate to approximately 17 billion pounds per year of unnecessarily trashed clothing, per the Environmental Protection Agency (EPA). The EPA's statistic means that every company, including both non-profit and for-profit clothing recyclers and donation centers, is included in the 15% of recycled textiles. Whether it be a monetary gift or clothing for resale, people looking to give to their favorite charity can and will continue to do so. Clothes Bin® is a *green,* for-profit recycling franchise whose opportunity is the billions of pounds of textiles *not* being recycled.

This is the story of how recycling met the need for unwanted clothing, shoes, and textiles and became a franchise opportunity named Clothes Bin®. When I first met with Marc Douglas, he had nearly 30-years of experience in the recycled clothing industry, including owning a group of thrift stores, wholesale purchasing, distribution and sales of used clothing, and running a public company in the industry. The concept of recycling clothing to reduce landfill waste while stimulating the economy by hiring employees, paying rental fees, and giving money to schools across the country, with an opportunity to generate income, was a breath of fresh air.

The Clothes Bin® mission is to help people reach their entrepreneurial dream of business ownership through a semi-absentee franchise system that promotes environmental stewardship, stimulates the economy, and provides a source of clothes, shoes, and textiles in the United States and throughout the world. Clothes Bin® isn't the next copycat or variation of another franchise brand that many of us see, with a different recipe and marketing pitch; this recycling opportunity was the groundwork for the industry's first textile recycling franchise. The Franchise Disclosure Document (FDD) started as a blank document and would require questioning, reasoning, insight and many hours to fill out the 23 standard items. We were, and are, fortunate to work with Robert Zarco's firm in Miami, Florida, as our general and franchise counsel, and specifically with their partner, Kaari Gagnon.

The Clothes Bin® team combines over 125 years of collection and distribution experience in the recycled textiles industry and franchise industry. We developed a proven process for the collection, management, and distribution of clothes, shoes, and textiles. The Bins are strategically located in the parking lots of convenience stores, gas stations, shopping centers, schools or wherever people congregate across the country.

Success! Or was it? Our plan was to put together the entire franchise system, and we accomplished that feat and were ready to go to market with the franchise system. This plan included the franchisor team, B.L.I.P.® (Bin Location Information Program) technology, online dashboard, analytics, telematics, marketing, mapping, financial structure, websites, creative and design, and legal documents, to name a few. In our first year of business, we generated $0 in revenue! We did not know who our target audience was, who our ideal franchisee would be or how to convey our opportunity in less than an hour, let alone the 15-30 second timeframe where you can keep someone's attention. But, we realized people understood our industry and what we did when they could see it in action, so we created a short whiteboard video that explained our franchise opportunity in less than three minutes.

One day, as I traveled to visit my parents, I checked my phone as I was walking off the plane. I saw a completed sign-up form from the Clothes Bin® website, an email from the same person, and a voicemail. Wow! But, here I was now in the car with my family on a three-hour drive. As much as this trip was to unwind and not work, my family obliged and, like it or not, was an audience to my call, and I was nervous. After about a two-hour call, I realized I was possibly speaking to our not-too-distant-future first franchisee. He let me know he did not want to work for corporate America any longer and did not want to be right-sized, up-sized, down-sized, or any other type of sized and not control his destiny. He wanted to be involved in a company with a *green initiative* and where he could grow into a full-time position. He wanted to feel more in control over his destiny.

At the beginning of any franchise system, the most challenging question to answer is, "How many franchisees do you have operating?" when the answer is "Zero." But, he took this fact as a positive opportunity, explaining he would receive all of the support as the first franchisee. As our talks progressed over the next few weeks, he let me know he wanted to buy six franchise territories. Six! To his disbelief and surprise, I countered with two territories, letting him know as the first franchisee, we needed to ensure he was successful and did not take on too much, too quickly. In the end, we agreed to award him with three franchise territories, but about nine months later, he did, in fact, purchase his 4th franchise territory and operates today with 160 Bins across those four territories, with over half of them located at schools.

How Does Clothes Bin® Work?

Bins are placed in ideal locations. We strategically look for locations in high-traffic areas, with great visibility of the Bin, and easy access to parking next to the Bin to place the clothing inside. We have written permission for the locations and offer to pay a fair rent.

Contributors fill the Bins. Our "customers" look for a convenient option to recycle their items. The large, galvanized steel Bins with *recycling green* powder-coated anti-graffiti paint are billboards helping direct recyclers to their location.

Service full Bins. Using B.L.I.P.® (Bin Location Information Program), our franchisees can monitor their fill levels of every Bin. The technology alleviates needing to aimlessly drive to Bins that may not be full, allows us to create an efficient route to service only the Bins approaching capacity, and use real-time mapping and turn-by-turn directions through a smartphone app for the drivers. The software tracks all locations' performance details and is used as a powerful tool for franchisee business reviews.

Unload contents. The clothing can be delivered directly to local buyers such as thrift stores, clothing recyclers, and wholesalers or loaded onto containers.

Receive funds for contents. The textiles are sold by the pound to buyers, whether it's a truck load or a trailer load.

Who wants someone's old, used and unwanted clothing? When you look at thrift stores supplied by Clothes Bin®, you may be surprised to see how many of the items arrive with their new sales tags still attached—clothing, shoes, and accessory items in dry cleaning bags and in perfect condition. Contributors of the Bins make a conscious effort to recycle their clothing and not throw them away, and many are neatly folded right from their dresser drawers or still on their closet hangers. One thing that differentiates Clothes Bin® is we *do* accept textiles in all conditions, so a ripped, stained, or faded garment can still be recycled through our process. Even when the condition is not suitable for a retail thrift store, these items can be bailed and recycled into wipe cloths, towels, and rags. The old worn-out shoes can be ground down into playground materials, packing materials, and other products.

The National Buyer Program is in place to assist franchisees with selling their collected, recycled textiles. A typical buyer may be a local thrift store or a regional or national wholesaler who grades and sorts the textiles. Clothes Bin® franchisees do *not* go through the clothing and try to pick out the best items. All deliveries are made to the buyers with the exact, original contributions made to their Bins. Many buyers are located domestically, but they also may have international operations where they supply thrift stores or wholesale markets around the world.

The majority of our current franchisees have other full-time jobs in addition to being a Clothes Bin® franchisee. As long as you have an internet connection, the Bins can be monitored and managed. We conduct two training programs for franchisees, including a two-day training program at our corporate headquarters in South Florida and a one-week training program in each franchisee's territory. Many franchisees choose to use our optional Bin Location Services to sign up locations for franchisees within their territory.

COVID-19 *The Pandemic*

Remember back in March 2020, the pandemic initiative "15 Days to Slow the Spread?" At the time of this writing, we are now more than nine months into the pandemic. Our corporate team took aggressive action in learning, watching, researching, and staying up to date with all COVID-19 related protocols. Effective Friday, March 13, 2020, our corporate office moved to 100% remote working. When I saw the "shelter in place" orders go into effect in California, we immediately worked on behalf of our franchisees to provide every one of them with their "Essential Recycling Business Package." We included the local, county and/or state mandates listing recycling as an *essential business*, as well as the latest safety guidelines.

I am so thankful to our remarkable team, who made sacrifices and worked extra hours throughout this process to assist our franchisees in any way possible while the world was rapidly changing. As the business closures intensified and spread throughout the entire country, we were ahead of this curve and provided every franchisee with this package, and no franchisee was forced to closed since we were, in fact, an *essential business*. Fortunately, our brand fits exceptionally well into the operating protocols of COVID-19, as our franchise model does not interact with the general public. We have one person in a truck servicing Bins where social distancing is not an issue.

While the country was shutting down, our Bins were still operating 24 hours per day. Even with "shelter in place, stay at home, and safer at home orders," our Bins at many locations across the country were located at essential businesses such as supermarkets and gas stations. Our model didn't feel the effects for almost two months after the pandemic was gaining steam, with May 2020 being our slowest month as retailers across the country were forced to close down or buyers had positive COVID-19 tests and needed to temporarily close. The Mexican and Canadian borders were both closed to regular travel, and to-date, have not reopened.

We let our franchisees know in March 2020, we would stop collecting royalties and B.L.I.P.® technology fees. We then forgave four months of technology fees and six months of royalties to assist franchisees regardless of their level of business interruption, as some franchisees were not dramatically affected. It ends up when people stay at home for long periods of time, that cleaning out their closets and recycling their clothes is on their to-do lists. In most areas around the country, our Bins filled faster during this time, as contributors did not need to worry about social interactions and social distancing when placing items into the Bins. During the pandemic, the National Buyer Program helped sell more than eight million pounds of recycled textiles, and in closing out the year, no franchisees were sitting on extra inventory.

Giving Back

Based on our Director of Marketing and Training, Chad Boariu's experience, we have partnered with hundreds of schools across the country where we pay for every pound of recycled textiles. Even though Clothes Bin® is a for-profit recycling franchise, which is clearly stated on each Bin, we have partnered with schools with our contactless Bins, where we provide them with educational materials about the importance of recycling textiles. These fundraising efforts are more crucial now that social distancing stopped other fundraisers such as bake sales and car washes. This program has raised hundreds of thousands of dollars, and during the pandemic, while schools were closed, they were still receiving monies for the recycled textiles.

Clothes Bin® is excited to continue growing through its franchise system and partnering with individuals looking for business ownership while not being required to leave their current work. This is the semi-absentee nature of our franchise system. We look forward to the upcoming years, innovations, working with our Franchise Advisory Council (FAC) members, meeting recycling objectives, and keeping clothing, shoes, and textiles out of local landfills. None of this would be possible without the support of our franchisees across the country and the exceptional staff I am proud and blessed to work with daily.

Chapter

Ten

1Heart Cares

Belina Calderon-Nernberg

Belina Calderon-Nernberg, CEO

1Heart Caregiver Service

Belina Calderon-Nernberg is an accomplished self-starter with over 25 years of business experience in Human Resources (HR) Recruitment and Senior Homecare Services combined. As the founder and CEO of a number of successful companies, one of which is 1Heart Caregiver Services, she provides the vision, leadership, and direction that her companies need to achieve their goals.

Belina's principle-centered leadership and ability to utilize corporate talents paved the way for the company to successfully achieve revenue, profit, and business growth objectives over the years.

This accomplishment has equipped 1Heart Caregiver Services with the expertise and proven systems to expand its business operations on a national level. Commencing in 2015, within a short period of time, 1Heart has rapidly expanded from a single office in Los Angeles to multiple locations in California and neighboring states.

Belina holds a Bachelor of Economics degree and is the recipient of numerous awards related to financial, business, and social services applications.

https://1heartcares.com/

https://1heartfranchise.com/

franchise@1heartcares.com

(818) 906-4441

1HEART CARES

By Belina Calderon-Nernberg

The Inception

I have always thought of financial freedom as a concept that is synonymous with the idea of the American dream. It is the reason why many immigrants like me take a leap of faith by leaving everything behind in the land of our birth and venturing into the land of opportunity.

I first came to visit the United States in the early '90s, at the young age of 24, newly married and pregnant with our first child. It didn't take long for me to fall in love again, this time, with a whole country—America, with its promise of a bright future for my family and me.

Armed with my bachelor's degree from the Philippines and my solid work ethic, I quickly found myself in the USCIS pipeline of skilled professionals who are qualified to become immigrants through employment. After 12 long years of working a nine-to-five job for a small cellular phone company in Encino, California, I had to accept the reality that I had reached the highest position that I could ever aspire for in the company. Having watched and learned from my bosses all those years in their business dealings, I finally realized that the best way for me to achieve my American dream of financial freedom was to do just what they were doing—run my own business.

As fate would have it, a simple act of helping one of my boss's relatives in finding a caregiver for his ailing dad paved the way to my eventually becoming a business owner—that of 1Heart Caregiver Services, an agency that provides personal and long-term, non-medical care to seniors and some adults with disabilities.

The Business Cycle and Its Potentials

1Heart's business operations are quite simple—recruit and hire caregivers, market and find clients, create the perfect match between the two, charge the client, pay the caregiver, and, repeat. As the saying goes, however, the devil is in the details, and all of these details will unfold as I continue my discussion below.

Since its inception in 2004, my caregiving business steadily grew as it built its reputation through satisfied clients, and I reveled in its success for the next decade. Unbeknownst to me at the time, however, I was only at the threshold of the senior care market as its exponential rise in the healthcare industry had only just begun.

The senior care market is primarily characterized by one particular demographic: the "baby boomers." From 1946 to 1964, roughly four million babies were born every year. At some point, the baby boomer generation composed about 40% of the total U.S. population and, inevitably, this demographic group caused an explosion in every market they touched. The rise in demand for consumer products, for the construction of new schools, the popularity of the music industry, and the ensuing suburban expansion can all be attributed to the effect this generation had on the economy as they grew older.

As these baby boomers approach their golden years, it is now apparent for the healthcare industry to experience immense growth. In the past two decades, Americans aged 65 years and older have grown from making up 12% to 16% of the total population. It is expected that almost 70% of these seniors will need home care at some point in their lives, and nine out of ten of them will want to stay at home. The demand for long term home care is, therefore, as inevitable as aging itself.

Why 1Heart?

A few years before I started the business, my mother, who lived in the Philippines, was diagnosed with cancer. Unfortunately, with 7,000 miles of ocean between us, I couldn't be there for her. The constraints brought about by my work responsibilities, and those of being a mom, wife and breadwinner for my family prevented me from being at her side to provide the support and care that she needed—mirroring a prevalent social dilemma where families with aging parents are forced by circumstances to live their lives away from mom and dad.

This firsthand knowledge of the stress and anxiety that come from being unable to personally care for an aging parent is one of the reasons why I established 1Heart, and I have resolved to make sure that 1Heart Caregiver Services not only provides quality care, but also gives peace of mind to every family that we serve. We have always held the highest standards for our staff and caregivers at 1Heart. All our caregivers undergo extensive criminal background checks, health screening, and training at our 1Heart Caregiver University prior to deployment in order to ensure that the best care possible is provided to our clients.

We offer a wide variety of services; some are more technical and focused on the client's health, like medication supervision, Alzheimer's care, and personal hygiene. Sometimes, our service could be as simple as companionship. It is truly amazing to see how something as simple as social interaction with a cheerful caregiver can make such a lasting impact on a senior who otherwise would be lonely, and stories abound of our caregivers having built meaningful relationships with their clients.

In California, 1Heart has maintained strict compliance with the rising standards of the Home Care Consumer Protection Act of 2016 that obligated every home care agency to create a policy of reporting elder abuse, required caregivers to complete five hours of annual training, that every caregiver pass a background check, and other pre-requisites designed to ensure the safety of the senior community. Unlike other agencies that had to be closed down due to non-compliance with this Act at the time, 1Heart never wavered in its mission and vision of upholding the highest standards of service and providing the highest degree of quality, reliable and compassionate care to our clients in the comfort of their home.

On a personal note, whenever I see the seniors under our care, I see myself at their age in their shoes, and I am reminded of my ultimate wish—to have someone like our caregivers take care of me in my own golden years.

Replicating through Franchising

After a decade of providing the 1Heart brand of service to the entire greater Los Angeles area in Southern California, I mulled over this idea of growing the business until I learned about franchising. I was intrigued by the idea of helping individuals who are yearning to build a business and fulfill their own American dreams the same way I did.

Through franchising, I thought I could replicate 1Heart's success several times over by advising and guiding others into building their own 1Heart Caregiver Services agency and using the 1Heart brand. In 2015, that thought became a reality when we opened our first franchise in Beverly Hills, California.

For us, each franchise not only opens up a great business opportunity, but also a chance to make a lasting impact on others. With each new franchisee that joins the team, we are able to make an even bigger impact. This type of franchise will not thrive if the owner is just looking to make money. It is a business that needs to be driven by a compassionate owner who is looking to make a difference in people's lives.

When applicants are considering the 1Heart franchise opportunity, there is a simple six-step process that every prospective franchisee goes through before being entrusted with holding and propagating the 1Heart brand and its core values.

First, we have them fill out a preliminary application form that allows us to assess whether they meet the basic requirements, as well as have the financial capability to fund this business venture.

Second, we have a meet-and-greet with the prospective franchisees to see if they are the right fit. The first thing that is asked of them is why they want to join our growing caregiving brand. We want to know the prospective applicant better—their traits, aspirations and what drives them—as every franchisee will become a standard-bearer of 1Heart.

It is imperative that we find franchisees who not only have what it takes to make their business flourish, but who could also properly represent and conduct themselves as a 1Heart agency. We look for individuals who have the drive to succeed, the compassion for the senior community, and are ready to faithfully follow the business model that the 1Heart team had developed through the years.

Third, we provide a Franchise Disclosure Document to the franchise applicant for their review. After 14 days, we meet to discuss all other questions that the applicant may have about the franchise contract details.

Fourth, we schedule Discovery Day at our corporate office, where the applicant gets an opportunity to meet our staff and executives, and see the business in operation.

If everything goes well, we're off to Contract Signing.

And finally, we go through an intensive five-day training at our headquarters to prepare the new franchisee in starting their 1Heart business. There are several phases of training that focus on knowledge and skills development in the different areas of sales, marketing, operations, and finance. There will also be periodic follow-up field training and business coaching in the franchisee's territory. Regular webinars and group training will also be conducted to ensure consistent business development and sustain efficient business operations.

1Heart will also provide a technology platform that will ensure the efficient running of the 1Heart system by providing accuracy in payroll, billing invoices, revenue, and gross profit analysis installed in the franchise's system.

The company has a solid area marketing and recruitment programs that help in business development and operations, together with a continuing professional education program and a health education advocacy.

An initial inventory of marketing collaterals with the 1Heart brand will also be provided.

Take it from a Franchisee

In the last five years since we first offered this opportunity to help people become their own boss, I have seen our franchisees create their own American story of success. We have franchisees who come from different backgrounds, such as seasoned business owners, long-time employees, young professionals, etc. But what impresses me the most are those who barely had the knowledge or experience in this business, but were courageous enough to take that leap of faith to invest everything they had in something that they believed could give them their American dream.

Take Raymond, for instance, a young man who came to this country with his young wife and son with barely enough money to sustain them for a few months. What he had, though, were big dreams and the determination to provide a good life for his family.

With just a little over two years of work experience in a family business, he had no healthcare background, and had never run his own business. He saw the huge potential of the

1Heart business model and, without hesitation, he invested all that he had saved up, and plunged into the role of being a business owner in an industry that he knew was bound to explode.

With due diligence and advice from our team, he picked a territory that was 80 miles from where he lived and committed to run the business well despite the distance he had to travel. By following the system and implementing the campaigns rolled out by the franchisor, he saw his business flourish.

A little over his third year into being his own boss, he opened up his second location in South Bay, California and bought his first investment property. Suffice it to say that he is well on his way to achieving his American dream.

This is what 1Heart is all about. We change people's lives.

Chapter

Oasis Senior Advisors
Tim Evankovich

Tim Evankovich, CEO
Oasis Senior Advisors

During his 25-year career as President and Co-Founder of The Cleaning Authority, Tim had the opportunity to develop an outstanding franchise organization from its inception to 185 locations in 42 states and Canada. He takes the reins of Oasis Senior Advisors with the experience and proven track record to promote a strong and successful business model. Already with 88 franchises, Tim realizes the vast growth and potential of this industry and foresees an immensely bright and promising future. With over 32 years in small business ownership, he knows what it takes to help franchisees become successful. In addition to his role as CEO of Oasis,

Tim also serves on the board of directors for the local Naples, FL chapter of the Chaine des Rotisseurs, as well as their Vice Echanshon. He is an active member of the International Franchise Association (IFA) and a frequent speaker for the IFA on Franchise Development.

www.oasissenioradvisors.com

tim@oasissenioradvisors.com

239-449-9292

OASIS SENIOR ADVISORS

By Tim Evankovich

Four thousand Americans turn 85 years old every day, and 7,000 turn 65. Baby boomers, the largest population group in history, turned 70 in 2016. That gives the senior living industry over 20 years of tremendous growth. Current statistics show that seven out of ten seniors will require some type of long-term care. The demand for assisted living (AL) continues to increase in exponential proportions, as evidenced by the constant building of AL communities. When we talk about an untapped market, you have to look at the breadth of the senior space. Calling it massive would be an injustice to the adjective.

Growing up in a small rural town in Ohio, I was blessed by having grandparents that lived into their 80s and 90s; one set impoverished immigrants from eastern Europe and the other a farmer and carpenter from the Pennsylvania Dutch area. They gave me a unique perspective on seniors at a very young age. For so many of us, getting a chance to grow up through our adolescence with our aging grandparents allowed us to reap the benefits of their wonderful wisdom and knowledge. It helped me to have a fond appreciation of our seniors; certainly, one of our nations' greatest natural resources and arguably one of our greatest untapped resources. I am also fortunate to still have my parents with me at 89 and 90 years old, respectively, so I've benefitted from yet another set of seniors to add another layer of life's experiences to my historical portfolio. For their age, my parents are in amazing health, so still enjoying the holidays with them is certainly a highlight for me annually. I am eternally grateful for the joys they provide and the laughter we share at every family gathering.

As I prepared to sell my first franchise organization, The Cleaning Authority, in 2013, I learned about this Oasis franchise opportunity. I have always been a believer that as you have been blessed, it's important to give back. This was just that opportunity, to not only help folks get into small business ownership, but the number of lives that our franchisees would touch on a daily, weekly, and monthly basis was heartwarming. It felt to me like I had come full circle, from relishing time with my grandparents, and then parents, to a business that puts our seniors on a pedestal.

Our seniors can offer us an abundance of experiences and history that can easily put us in awe of their life's events and encounters. We marvel at their memories of world wars and world events from their childhood perspectives. We bask in their glow as they share with excitement the emotions they felt as they watched men land on the moon and the Beatles appear on Ed Sullivan for the first time. So, when people ask me what got me into the senior space, and I look at my background, and it becomes very apparent: The love of my ancestors and all that they have done to help me get to where I am today. As the CEO of Oasis Senior Advisors, not only do I have the opportunity to help people get into small business ownership and help them achieve their lifelong goals, but I also get the gratification of knowing the number of seniors and their families that our advisors touch every day. It is inspiring.

Another important factor to remember about our baby boomers is they were products of parents who lived through the Great Depression. Thus, they tended to be savers. As they grew to retirement, they had the resources to afford higher levels of retirement options. That is why the need for Oasis Senior Advisors is so significant. Those options can be mountainous, and they need an experienced, trusted resource to help them navigate those waters. When one of our advisors tells a family and their senior that they will have the financial resources to afford a beautiful, assisted living community and be very well taken care of, the family is truly overjoyed. You can literally see the stress just roll off their faces.

Our advisors provide a free service to seniors and their families, assisting them in finding the perfect assisted living or memory care community for their elderly loved ones. This is a very challenging and difficult time for the family as they make that tough decision to place their parent into assisted living. This is also a very emotional decision to make, typically by the children of the senior. This always leads to second-guessing their choice as to whether it was the right move. Our advisors expertly guide the family, helping them fully understand all the options available to them.

So often, when the family is in this situation, they don't know where to turn. There are countless options and so many variables to consider: diagnosis, prognosis, short and long-term help required, financial situation, lifestyle, geographic location, and many more. We help them step by step. Our advisors remove the stress and fear from the family, allowing them to focus on the wellbeing of their senior. This is really the mission of Oasis Senior Advisors: To put the needs of the senior at the forefront of the decision process. As you can imagine, this is a feel-good franchise. All our advisors do is help people!

Oasis Senior Advisors is a relationship-driven business. Our advisors build relationships in three distinct areas. Certainly, the seniors and their families are our focus and the paramount relationship that is built. Our franchisees also develop strong relationships with the assisted living, memory care and other senior living communities in their territory. However, the most crucial relationships are with the other geriatric and senior industry professionals in their area. These include both medical and non-medical professionals. As an example, they will foster strong connections with case managers, social workers, discharge planners, concierge doctors and estate planners. Anyone who is commonly the first or second line of defense and realizes a senior may need additional support are our key partners. They are looking out for the safety and security of that senior.

The franchisees of Oasis Senior Advisors are truly appreciated by three groups of relationships they build. First, the senior and the family love them because the advisor provides them a free service with options, information, and resources that enables them to make decisions during a difficult and challenging time. Second, the assisted living and memory care communities love them because they help seniors who are the right fit for their community connect with them. Third, the professionals providing services to seniors trust in their partnership with our advisors. The constant communication and coordination ensure that the seniors and their families receive the support they need. Truly, a feel-good franchise.

Oasis Senior Advisors looks for franchisees who genuinely like people and who enjoy meeting new people. Our strongest franchisees love to network and build solid relationships with industry professionals. They have a desire to help people and have a compassionate heart. We commonly hear our candidates say they are ready for the next chapter in their life, and they want an opportunity to give back. They want to make a difference in peoples' lives, and they want to be part of the fabric of their community. Many have done the corporate gig for many years, and now they want a chance to help change lives.

One of the many amazing stories from our franchisees is about an elderly couple in their late 80s. The loving husband was trying unsuccessfully to take care of his ailing wife when the family decided they needed to be separated as she was placed in assisted living. The Oasis advisor helped place the wife in a beautiful, assisted living community while the husband remained in their home. Knowing the husband was weak from caring for his frail wife, our compassionate advisor kept tabs on him over the course of the next few days. Upon arriving at his house one morning to check on him, he did not answer the door. Police were called to enter the home only to find him lying on the floor, unable to move. He had been lying there for many hours. Dehydrated and extremely weak, our advisor was able to get him to the hospital and eventually into assisted living with his wife. Had it not been for the dedication, focus and commitment of our franchisee, the couple would not have been able to celebrate another wedding anniversary a few weeks later.

The family of the seniors were greatly appreciative of our advisor and were truly touched by the advisor's concern for their parents.

Stories like this are frequent from our advisors because they tend to go above and beyond the concept of a "senior placement agent." One of the many ways we effectively help our families and their seniors, is by utilizing our OasisIQ™ proprietary software. This software helps match the senior to the right assisted living community using multiple factors, including budget, geography, and healthcare needs. OasisIQ™ provides significant time savings for the franchisee and removes any subjectivity, ensuring that thc advisor considers each of the communities that could be a great fit for the senior as they are identifying options for the family. OasisIQ™ provides a backbone for our advisors' business. The HIPAA compliant, web-based software platform provides our franchisees access to all of their data from any internet-accessible device, with functionality for community matching, referrals to both community and non-community partners, and invoicing. This enables them to be very agile and mobile throughout their busy day.

A franchisee begins their training as an Oasis Senior Advisor with initial five-day training in Bonita Springs, Florida. We also require at least one owner of each franchise to become a Certified Senior Advisor®, a trusted senior industry certification whose extensive ethics program aligns with our own OSA ethics pledge. The five-day initial training focuses on learning the core principles of the Oasis business model, the senior industry, OasisIQ™, marketing strategies, plus a day out in the field. The training is very comprehensive, and franchisees leave with a great comfort level to start their business.

The initial training is followed by a ten-week program that emphasizes and revisits key principles just as they are needed when ramping up their business. Continued training is provided monthly, both in operations and marketing and at our annual convention.

Our franchisees embrace the idea of a home-based business with low monthly overhead costs. They appreciate the scalability of Oasis and the opportunity to build a very lucrative business. In 2020, our top three franchisees averaged over $700,000 gross revenue. Our top five franchisees averaged over $600,000 gross revenue and our top ten averaged over $440,000 gross revenue. The low overhead costs enable our franchises to recognize profit and gives them the ability to reinvest profits into their business. They also appreciate the strong support network that is provided by the corporate office, including a large marketing department and strong operations team. Currently, 75% of the operations team are previous franchisees of Oasis, bringing their first-hand experience to the team. Finally, OasisIQ™ enables them to manage their business efficiently and effectively and positions them to increase the volume of referrals they can manage day to day.

The cost to be part of Oasis Senior Advisors is very affordable. We are considered a low investment franchise, typically under $100,000. This investment also includes your training, operational manual suite, a start-up marketing program and the proprietary OasisIQ™ software. It also includes our amazing operational support program, which is second-to-none in the industry.

If you feel Oasis Senior Advisors may be a great fit for you, we welcome the opportunity to take you through our exploratory process to find out if you're a great fit for our team. Please contact me at tim@oasisenioradvisors.com or 239-449-9292.

We look forward to starting your journey to small business ownership.

Chapter
Twelve

Franchising For Good
Jeff Hughes

Jeff Hughes
Skill Samurai

Jeff was born and raised in Brantford, Ontario, and now lives in Moncton, New Brunswick, with his wife, Sarah, and their three children. At a young age, he began traveling the world doing relief work. He has worked with marginalized women in the Philippines and juvenile delinquents in Russia. In 1994 Jeff was recognized by the United States Congress for his work among juvenile delinquents in Moscow. Jeff brings a background in business ownership, marketing and teaching. Jeff was a top three finalist for the 2010 Canadian Pizza Chef of the year, as decided by Canadian Pizza magazine. (Yes, there is a Canada Pizza magazine.)

His articles have been featured in national magazines. Through his work with non-profit organizations, Jeff has two decades of experience recruiting and training teams.

In 2015 Jeff founded Level UP Learning, Inc., with the goal of becoming a leader in the enrichment education market. Level UP Learning, Inc. sells franchises under the Level UP Kids and Skill Samurai brands.

www.skillsamurai.com

franchising@skillsamurai.com

https://www.linkedin.com/in/jefferydhughes

506-899-3788

FRANCHISING FOR GOOD
PREPARING CHILDREN FOR TOMORROW'S WORKPLACE, WHILE HELPING YOU BUILD A BRIGHT FINANCIAL FUTURE.

By Jeff Hughes

Industry

If you're a parent of a school-age child, or if you've spent any time in the education industry, you have undoubtedly heard a great deal about STEM. This snappy acronym combining Science, Technology, Engineering, and Mathematics has been on the tip of everyone's tongue in the education and tutoring industries for several years now, and it doesn't seem to be going anywhere soon. While it may seem like just the latest buzzword in education right now, STEM instruction is absolutely vital to the future success of the next generation, as we continue to prioritize technology in workplaces across multiple industries.

Despite the genuine importance of STEM-based education and the enthusiasm embraced by parents and teachers alike, not much is being done within a typical school curriculum to teach foundational technology concepts or provide adequate skillsets for career-readiness in our changing marketplace. Some supplemental education franchises offer STEM courses designed to expand students' exposure to key concepts and generate interest for tech-based games, lessons, and activities. However, only Skill Samurai goes beyond the typical after-school STEM classes that are offered to school-age children by ensuring that actual tech skills are being learned. Through proven courses and programs designed to engage, entertain, and spark interest, children get hands-on experience with real programming languages and software applications that are used in many IT-based fields, including coding, game development, and artificial intelligence (AI).

While STEM is having a moment as the “it” topic in children’s education, it is far more than just a trend for parents and teachers; however, as Skill Samurai franchise owners can attest, the buzz around STEM doesn’t exactly hurt business either. Our franchise owners are uniquely positioned to capitalize on the excitement around STEM while providing the children in their community with the tools they need to succeed in virtually any career path they choose. A rewarding, lucrative career that helps to prepare our future generation for success is possible when you become a Skill Samurai.

The world has changed, and so has the way that people work and are trained for work. Millions of jobs that existed for previous generations have been lost to automation, downsizing and globalization.

85% of the jobs that will exist in 2030 haven’t been created yet. Our schools aren’t teaching the skills that kids will need. At Skill Samurai, our STEM curriculum and face-to-face coding classes equip kids with life skills to help them thrive both now and in the future.

Skill Samurai resides within three distinct industries (education and tutoring, summer camps, and birthday parties) with a combined and steady growth of $131 billion annually. Parents prioritize their children’s future success through education, so these industries are also *recession resilient*. Because of the way technology is replacing jobs with computers at an increasing rate, the need for STEM programs is not going to slow down anytime soon.

Education and tutoring - $102.8 Billion

Summer camps - $3 Billion

Birthday parties - $25 Billion

Background

When it comes to computer science, you can say I was "late to the party." I didn't begin learning essential and valuable skills such as programming until well into adulthood, as it became apparent that a solid IT foundation was absolutely necessary for my future career success. My late entry into computer science made me think about my own three young kids and how an earlier introduction to the STEM disciplines could not only spark an interest in exciting technologies in emerging fields but also help them gain a competitive edge and set them up for bright, successful careers straight out of college.

After doing a little research in my native Canada, I was shocked to find that the application of technology in elementary school instruction was virtually nonexistent at many schools. Despite the number of great teachers working in the public school system, the curriculum was simply not geared toward serving the glaring gaps in the vital STEM fields. Case in point—at my children's school, which has a student body of 300, only three computers were available for student use! It became clear that there was an unmet need for in-school STEM instruction that would adequately prepare students for future career opportunities as emphasis continues to be placed on advancing tech across virtually all industries. How were these kids going to be able to learn the skills they would need to compete in the workplace of the future?

In 2014, I decided to take matters into my own hands by creating an education industry-leading concept that would provide children and teens with a STEM curriculum focused on career-readiness through a better understanding of technology. We offered after-school programs and camps featuring a variety of proven, interactive, hands-on educational courses that seamlessly blended fun and learning.

Services

With declining supply and increasing demand, Skill Samurai is in a unique position to fill this unmet need. With multiple, complementary revenue streams, Skill Samurai taps into three growth segments within the children's services space:

Children's Education and Tutoring

STEM enrichment programs are currently a combined $130 billion industry, and those numbers are projected to increase over the next several years. The children's education and tutoring industry, specifically, is $7 billion, and is referred to as a "recession-resistant industry."

Summer/School Vacation Camps

Summer and school vacation camps are often dismissed as a low-revenue segment, but data proves otherwise. In the U.S., parents spend over $4 billion a year on sending their kids to camps, including STEM education programs.

Birthday Parties

Every child has a birthday, and parents are increasingly looking into innovative and unique ways to celebrate. Now a $5 billion industry, birthday parties at STEM education franchises like Skill Samurai are becoming big business as parents continue to seek higher value and more diverse options for their children.

Additional Revenue Streams

After-school programs, camps, and parties are just some of the many revenue streams supported by the Skill Samurai business model. We feature a number of additional classes and activities, including Parents' Night Out, competitive leagues, and college internships, to create consistent, recurring streams of revenue that complement one another, adding to the franchise owner's bottom line.

Course Content Makes Learning Fun

As any parent can tell you, it can be a struggle to get kids to do things that will benefit their education in the long run. Here at Skill Samurai, we understand that the best way to teach children the concepts that will prepare them for future success is by turning learning into a game! We achieve this by incorporating popular games like Fortnite, Minecraft, and Roblox into our curriculum to introduce students to real-world programming languages.

Our commitment to effectively preparing young people for future careers in STEM-based disciplines extends beyond what students learn in their Skill Samurai courses. Skill Samurai is the only education franchise that offers industry-recognized certification exams. The Skill Samurai program combined with certification gives students the opportunity to enter the workforce with on-the-job experience in their chosen field, something that will immediately set them apart from the fierce competition when they apply for post-college jobs.

Franchise Opportunity

If you've read this far and feel like the Skill Samurai opportunity is perfect for you, great! We're seeking a certain type of franchise owner to carry the Skill Samurai brand to communities around the world. Our most successful franchise owners possess the following characteristics:

Passion for technology

At Skill Samurai, we believe that anything is achievable through technology, and we want franchise owners who not only share our passion for computer science, IT, and other tech-oriented concepts, but are also able to pass it on to their customers.

Growth mindset

Technology is always changing, and Skill Samurai franchise owners must be able to change with it. Our ideal owners exhibit a readiness to scale their business.

Sales and marketing-oriented

We are seeking franchise owners with a background in business, preferably with experience in sales or marketing.

Networking know-how

Are you an active participant in your community? Do you have an "in" with local schools, recreation centers, or other youth-focused programs? We find that franchise owners who can effectively network with other businesses are the most accomplished at effectively building their customer base.

If your ideals, values, and beliefs about the importance of STEM education in children's lives are in alignment with ours, and you are excited about the possibility of providing kids in your community with a next-level foundation in STEM education, we want to talk.

Skill Samurai is proud to offer comprehensive support for new and existing franchise owners.

What's included:

A comprehensive start-up plan

Let's be honest; if you're successful, then so are we. We will bend over backward to support your new business.

Owners receive:

80 hours of training

STEM.org certification

Pre-launch support

Weekly coaching calls

Annual regional conferences

Franchise growth manager

You'll have access to your own business coach. You'll learn best-practices and avoid some of the typical mistakes that most new franchisees make.

Curriculum Development

We are working tirelessly behind the scenes to develop new courses to keep students engaged and keep pace with technology.

Business Management Technology

Technology and systems are required for success, but it can be daunting starting.

from scratch. No worries! Websites, social,, booking software, CRM, and marketing—we've got you covered.

Marketing support

Our marketing support team helps you promote upcoming classes, camps, and events through various web and social media channels. We have developed a variety of advertising materials and sales aids to make things easier!

A powerful and supportive network

The power of a franchise group lies in its franchisees. We believe that culture is important. When you join Skill Samurai, you'll join a supportive network of ethical, like-minded entrepreneurs.

One of our main marketing activities is partnering with schools to offer after-school coding and robotics classes. One of our first attendees was Eleanor. She was five years old when she brought home one of our flyers. She said, "Mom, I am five years old, and I don't know how to code yet." Her mom signed her up! Eleanor is now ten, and she has been in our programs every year. Her parents saw the passion that her daughter had, and our programs were a way for them to encourage Eleanor's love of computers.

We believe that whether or not Eleanor pursues coding as a career, we can provide her with the skills that will help her pursue her dreams.

Are you looking for a career change that offers the right balance of security, mental challenge and financial upside? We understand that changing careers can be daunting. You deserve a proven, flexible franchise that has a positive impact while helping you build a bright financial future.

Franchise owners love the flexibility that Skill Samurai offers them:

"It gave me the flexibility to be my own boss, to spend more time with my family, and still do what I needed to do during the day, as the classes were in the evening. If you are looking for something easy, flexible, and fun, then this is the way to go. You not only do it for yourself, but also do it for the community by preparing kids for the future."

Chapter

Thirteen

A Unique B2B Franchise
Jayesh Kasim

Jayesh Kasim.

Valenta BPO Solutions

As the founder and Managing Director of Valenta BPO Solutions, my priority is to ensure we offer our clients the most effective and efficient solutions for their business operations.

Valenta BPO is a process consulting, digital transformation and outsourcing business with offices in Australasia, North America, United Kingdom and operational centers in India and Malaysia.

We work with businesses globally to identify process improvements, implement bespoke technology, and deliver outsourcing services.

I enjoy meeting our existing and prospective clients. For our existing clients, my priority is to ensure we are delivering our service beyond expectations and identifying areas of process improvement. For our prospective clients, my priority is to understand their current systems and processes and provide solutions that would enable them to grow their business beyond what it would otherwise achieve. With active engagement, we are able to refine our processes and ensure our clients are receiving the highest quality and value.

I'm actively involved in our franchise recruitment to ensure we build a strong network of franchise partners globally. I work with each franchise partner on a strategic level to help them build success in their business.

Our approach is to add value to our clients and assist in their business growth. This enables us to build and develop long-term relationships.

www.valentabpo.com

jayesh.kasim@valentabpo.com

877 568 1035

A UNIQUE B2B FRANCHISE

By Jayesh Kasim

When people think of franchising, they think of brick-and-mortar stores. However, there are plenty of opportunities available besides the brick and motor stores. One of those is B2B Franchises, which are professional and sophisticated. Most corporate executives feel comfortable operating in a professional environment, and that's exactly what a B2B Franchise offers.

2020 has re-set businesses globally. Over the next three to five years, businesses are going to think about new operating models. They are going to think about staffing, office space, infrastructure, travel, marketing, and the like. Digital transformation/automation was good to have prior to Covid-19, and now it's a must for every business to survive and become more profitable.

Research indicates that 90% of businesses struggle to implement digital transformation projects in-house, and this is due to the knowledge gap. This is where digital transformation companies thrive and provide business a full end to end solutions, from consulting, implementation to training.

At Valenta, we offer businesses three key services:

Consulting

Digital Transformation

Outsourcing

Valenta started in 2014 as an outsourcing business wherein we provided virtual staff to businesses. The staffing was for various positions such as accounting, software development, marketing, and so on. The benefits of this included cost-effective staff, not having to deal with HR issues, getting things done quicker or overnight, to name a few. By 2016, we realized the need for businesses to have the right processes in place to take advantage of outsourcing, and with this, we launched our *Process Consulting* service. Our process consultants are from the likes of KMPG, EY, and others, and as such, we are able to provide a high level of service without the price tag. Most recently, in 2020, we launched our *Digital Transformation* service wherein we look at processes that are repetitive and manual in nature and automate them using robotic process automation and artificial intelligence.

On the consulting front, we offer our clients an *Operational Analysis* to identify gaps and provide them a roadmap.

On the automation front, we offer our clients *Proof of Concept* wherein we automate one business process for them to understand the impact.

We can engage with businesses via any one of our services and, over time, offer them a holistic solution and improve efficiencies.

Our franchise partners take a consultative sales approach. They identify businesses, work with the C-Level or Management team in understanding pain points and the vision, and ultimately provide solutions using our services.

Our franchise partners are supported by experts in consulting, digital transformation, and outsourcing and, as such, don't need to be experts in these areas.

We find most of our successful franchisees possess the following skills:

Consultative sales experience

Excellent communication/relationship building skills

Strong business acumen

Pro-active attitude

Leadership skills

Customer-centric

High emotional intelligence

A track record of success

We provide our franchise partners extensive support and work together as a team. This includes:

Business planning

Sales coaching

Marketing support

IT support

Annual conference

We understand everyone has different goals. Once we understand what each one wants to achieve, we work with them in providing strategic advice to achieve their goals.

We have a one-month onboarding process, which includes one to two meetings each day. Towards the end of this process, we work on a three-page business plan, and more importantly, we review it every three months.

During the on-boarding process, our franchise partners meet key people within the business, including our marketing team. Our marketing team works very closely with each one to understand their target market and prepare the marketing collateral they need.

We have a panel of sales coaches that our franchise partners can choose to work with. Each of our sales coaches has been highly successful and understands our business. They can provide as much support as required.

Our technology stack lets our franchise partners operate effectively from anywhere. We use a Zoho CRM across the business, Lucid Press for marketing, Sales Genie for business data, and others. We review our technology stack from time to time.

As we don't have a brick-and-mortar requirement, our franchise partners can be up and running within four to six weeks. They can commence working from home or a service office.

We have three monthly fees: $800 for marketing, $200 for IT, and $100 for the annual conference.

The cost of operating our franchise can vary based on the business goals and structures. It's possible for an owner-operator to start the business with a monthly recommended marketing budget of $1,000, while it's also possible for a franchise owner to hire a team of sales consultants and have a much higher marketing budget.

Our model is designed for our franchise partners to work *on* their business rather than *in* their business by taking care of the service delivery while our franchise partners maintain the client relationship and project manage the services at a high level.

We have franchise partners with diverse backgrounds. We have everyone from lawyers, army pilots, sales directors, and digital transformation consultants, to our youngest franchise partner being a graduate from University.

Ten percent of our franchise partners are under 30. With our support and their ambition, we are able to make them successful business owners.

Prior to starting Valenta, I was a franchise owner of a financial services franchise. I started with one franchise in 2010 and opened two more locations over a period of three years. I set up a back-office team when I started my first franchise. The back office helped us with processing work a lot faster, and we were able to re-invest the savings into local area marketing and recruiting sales staff to look after customers. This strategy helped us open the next two offices. By 2014, I realized the back office was our key to success, and hence I decided to sell my three franchises and start Valenta in 2014 to offer services to SME's globally.

Prior to franchising Valenta in 2019, we proved the model globally. Initially starting in Australia in 2014, expanding to the U.K. in 2016, U.S. in 2017 and Canada and New Zealand in 2018. During this period, we realized business requirements and the decision-making process was the same globally. Using my prior experience as a franchisee, I decided to take the best part of franchising and combined it with our services to offer the unique franchise opportunity of Valenta.

If you are passionate about helping other businesses and want to take control of your lifestyle, I highly encourage starting as early as possible and giving it everything you have.

Chapter

Fourteen

It's All About The
Wedding Dress
Chris and Winnie Lee

Chris and Winnie Chlomin Lee

Winnie Couture

Winnie Couture was founded by the husband-and-wife team of Chris and Winnie Chlomin Lee. Serving as CEO, Chris leads the sales and operational side of the business, while Winnie brings her talents to the role of Creative Director and Lead Designer. This power couple is the epitome of what everyone desires in their personal and professional relationships.

With over 20 years of experience in executive and supply chain management, Chris is familiar with all aspects of the wedding industry. Winnie brings her vision and incomparable creativity to the business. With a love for design, an obsession for detail, and a passion for perfection, her works are synonymous with modern elegance. Her creations have graced the covers of magazines, wowed at celebrity weddings, and walked the red carpet to the click of cameras. Carrie Underwood, Kelly Clarkson, Jennifer Aniston, Lea Michele, Taraji P. Henson, and Helen Hunt are just some of the famous names that have worn her dresses.

Winnie's works have also been featured on the hottest TV shows, including ABC's The Bachelorette, Netflix's Fuller House, FOX's GLEE, NBC's Miss Universe, Bravo's The Real Housewives, and many more.

In just 20 years, Chris and Winnie Lee have taken a small business and turned it into an internationally recognized brand in the $70 billion bridal wear industry. Their hard work and dedication have also enabled them to empower others through franchising opportunities. Now entrepreneurs can take advantage of the Winnie Couture brand by owning a high-profit margin luxury bridal salon.

Want freedom, flexibility, financial security and the ability to leave a legacy? Contact Chris today for franchising opportunities and business consultation.

www.winniecouture.com

chris@winniecouture.com

IG: WinnieCouture

310-882-8889

IT'S ALL ABOUT THE WEDDING DRESS

By Chris and Winnie Lee

For couples, there's no occasion more memorable or anticipated than their wedding day. With 2.1 million Americans tying the knot every year, couples spend a total of $52 billion on wedding-related expenses—venues, flowers, photography, music, catering—no cost is too great.

The bridal industry is rarely affected by politics, pandemics, or economics. Couples are finding ways to celebrate love, no matter the circumstances. In fact, reports indicate that the wedding dress market is poised for massive growth over the next five years. That's because the wedding gown is a once-in-a-lifetime splurge item, as well as the centerpiece of every wedding. It symbolizes beauty, elegance and femininity—the one piece of clothing that catches every eye and takes away everyone's breath.

Despite the rise of online shopping, the experience of finding *the* dress at a brick-and-mortar store is something brides will always cherish. There's nothing like going to the bridal salon with your family and best friends, trying on dress after dress, and finding the one that's right for you. Just as every bride says yes to that special someone, they also say yes to that perfect dress.

Starting a wedding gown business is both lucrative and extremely rewarding. To see the sheer joy *the* dress can bring a woman and be part of that moment—who wouldn't want to do that for a living?

Fashion Meets Passion

Winnie Couture was born when the company's founders were planning their own nuptials. The outpouring of love from the wedding community sparked their desire to bring joy to other couples. In fact, it's been said the company is as old as Chris and Winnie's marriage.

But the founders realized that the industry lacked a private environment where women could freely express themselves in the presence of those they trusted most. So, in addition to gorgeous wedding attire, they created intimate bridal dreamlands where women felt loved and supported while saying *yes* to their dream dress.

Chris and Winnie's goal was simple: to combine fashion-forward wedding apparel with customized solutions and a personalized shopping experience.

Since then, the brand has gained a worldwide following, with a network of famous celebrities, producers, and influencers as fans. Driven by a team of talented, empowered women, the company now boasts over 150 authorized retailers, seven flagship stores, and three franchise locations, having served over a quarter of a million brides!

The future is bright for the Winnie Couture brand—and its investors.

The Experience of a Lifetime

Finding a wedding dress should be serene, not stressful.

With that mantra in mind, Winnie Couture has created a shopping experience, unlike any other. When brides-to-be walk into our boutiques, they're greeted with a glass of champagne and a friendly bridal stylist. Every Winnie Couture salon is meticulously designed from top to bottom, decked out in chic chandeliers, gleaming floors and ornate décor.

In short: the entire atmosphere is one of luxury, romance, and queenly comfort.

We also make it fun to find the perfect dress with the aid of our expert staff. Our bridal stylists offer helpful guidance based on factors like wedding theme, body type, budget, the bride's vision, and how she wants to feel on her special day.

After the initial consultation, our stylists take the bride to a private suite to discuss the details of her dream dress. Necklines, silhouettes, colors, fabrication, and more—we clarify your vision of the perfect gown.

There are so many varieties of dresses that brides struggle finding. It's almost like preparing your first ever Thanksgiving dinner for your in-laws all by yourself. The following bride-to-be comes to mind.

The day before July 4th, Caroline walked into Winnie Couture's Beverly Hills location with her mother, sister, and maid of honor. She had already visited eight other salons and left feeling disappointed that she had yet to find "the dress." With her wedding just months away, and her mother and sister only in town for a week from Arizona, Caroline was understandably anxious. However, she decided to make an appointment after seeing some stylish pics on our website and real weddings on our Instagram.

Once here, Caroline explained she wanted a mermaid dress, but was otherwise a "blank canvas" and open to suggestions. Amanda, our bridal stylist, pulled Tilda, Stefanie, Tallulah, Tinsley, and Londyn dresses from Caroline's My Closet feature on our website. She also extracted a Hermione gown based on their consultation.

Caroline looked amazing in everything she wore, but she looked most beautiful in the Stefanie and the Hermione. Amanda had a feeling that the Hermione was going to be *the* dress by the smile on Caroline's face. The Hermione gown featured spaghetti straps and a modified sweetheart neckline, which elongated her torso and accentuated her silhouette. Amanda then added a matching fingertip length organza veil, a pair of dangling white crystal rhodium-plated earrings, and a Seraphina belt.

Struck speechless at the sight of herself in the grand mirror, Caroline loved how her shoulders and upper body appeared in the dress. She exuded beauty and radiated confidence.

Teary-eyed, the entire bridal party knew Caroline had found her dream dress.

Amanda, presenting Caroline a white rose bouquet and leading her around by the hand, asked:

"Do you feel as beautiful as you look?" asked Amanda.

Caroline smiled.

"Do you feel like a bride?"

Smiling angelically, Caroline nodded.

"Are you saying *yes* to the dress?" asked Amanda.

"Yes!" the bride-to-be exclaimed.

"Woohoo! You're a Winnie Bride now! Let's celebrate!" declared Amanda.

Suddenly the whole bridal party erupted into cheers and celebrations.

Amanda shared in their joy. She wasn't just a bridal stylist—she was a dream-maker.

Afterward, Caroline posed for photos with an "I SAID YES" sign.

She had entered Winnie Couture, anxious and disappointed. She left elated and overjoyed with her dream dress.

The Winnie Couture Franchise Experience

To celebrate their son Athan's 9th birthday, Chris and Winnie spent a spontaneous night at Disney's Grand California Hotel and Spa, a mere 30-minute drive from their home. During dinner, the couple discussed the exceptional customer service they had received. From the warm welcome of Athan's favorite Disney character (the Genie from Aladdin) to the tour guide, everyone they met was friendly, welcoming and professional. Even the hotel rooms were magnificently detailed, with murals above the headboards depicting characters like Bambi.

The result: every customer—child or adult—was ecstatic to be there.

This led Chris and Winnie to an inspirational idea...why not bring this ultimate VIP experience to other cities?

"It would be really amazing to offer the Hollywood styles and the Winnie experience to every hometown, so the brides and their family and friends don't have to travel very far to visit us!" said Chris.

With stores across the country from Beverly Hills to Boston, our aim was to create a universal "Winnie Couture experience" no matter the location. Over time, we created a proven process for scaling this experience so others could follow.

The Winnie Couture franchise was developed to share our knowledge, resources and expertise with passionate entrepreneurs. Our goal is to help people build their dream business and enjoy the freedom, fulfillment and financial security it brings.

Take Courtney, one of our franchisees.

The moment she stepped into our upscale salon as a bride-to-be, she knew she wanted to be part of the Winnie Couture family. Years later, when Courtney found out we were offering franchising opportunities, she immediately jumped at the chance.

Her passion grew with every step of the franchising process. Starting with the brand overview call, she discovered the story behind the Winnie Couture brand—our mission and core values. By the end of that call, Courtney knew she was the ideal franchisee candidate.

In her words, "OMG! This describes me perfectly!"

During the operations interview, Courtney fantasized about the day-to-day processes of running a luxury bridal salon. She quickly grasped Winnie Couture's easy-to-follow system and loved our strong industry presence and international name recognition.

When Courtney visited our flagship location in Atlanta for a discovery day, she remembered how she felt walking into our store as a bride-to-be. The chandelier above, the champagne glass in her hand, surrounded by her best friends—the feelings came rushing back.

She met our operations manager, Jennifer, who gave her a tour of the salon. Courtney enjoyed every moment of it, from the luxurious atmosphere of her surroundings to the incomparable artistry of Winnie's designs.

Her favorite moments came when observing the brides themselves. She could sense their excitement, see the passion and dedication of the stylists who attended them, and shared in their jubilation when a bride finally screamed yes to the dress!

Just as those brides had found their perfect dress, Courtney knew she had found the business of her dreams. She was saying yes to being a Winnie Couture franchisee.

After her life-changing decision, Courtney began the site selection process, settling on Nashville—the bachelorette capital of the world. Six months later, with the help and guidance of Winnie Couture's franchise development team, Courtney's dream came true. She now had her very own Winnie Couture store!

The romantic radiance of the chandeliers, the plush décor, the intimate fitting rooms, the Swarovski elements emanating from the couture gowns, and the overwhelming sense of luxury and comfort—this shimmering bridal dreamland was hers and every bride-to-be who walked through the front door.

"We are excited to be opening in Nashville and for Winnie Couture becoming an essential part of the community,"

Courtney told the Nashville press. "It is our desire to be a brand woven into the fabric of what makes Nashville great!"

COVID-19 And A Brighter Future

The pandemic has interrupted every aspect of our lives. Weddings are no exception. Countless couples have been forced to pause their wedding plans or push back the dates indefinitely. Some couples have opted for smaller and more intimate ceremonies, while others have postponed their special day till restrictions are lifted.

Despite the fear and uncertainty, couples are still planning on getting married. According to The Wedding Report, 2021 is expected to see an unprecedented surge in weddings. Whereas 1.1 million Americans were married in 2020, that number is set to hit 2.77 million next year!

The pandemic has created a craving for normalcy and tradition, and nothing says tradition like weddings—or wedding dresses.

With vaccines already being distributed throughout the country, next year will see a tidal wave of marriages. The $70 billion bridal wear industry is set to explode. That means there's no better time to be a part of the wedding industry or a Winnie Couture franchisee.

If you've ever dreamed of starting your own business, being an entrepreneur, taking control of your life and finances, or following your passion and leaving a legacy—this is the opportunity you've been waiting for!

Chapter *Fifteen*

The Best Opportunity You've Never Thought Of

Paul Linenberg

Paul Linenberg

Gotcha Covered

Paul has been the President of Gotcha Covered since 2010, following a varied career in sales, marketing, and entrepreneurship. Paul excels at being lucky, especially in being able to work with an amazing group of people at Gotcha Covered and helping provide custom window treatments for people across the U.S. and Canada.

Paul grew up in the Detroit area, and his love of the Red Wings has never wavered. He graduated from Miami (of Ohio) and has had to explain that several hundred times over the years. Paul has been in Colorado since 2000.

Paul plays hockey, practices Krav Maga, and occasionally gets behind his drum set to fill the house with slightly off-tempo, but incredibly enthusiastic heavy metal drum covers. Also, a fan of craft beer and not cooking, Paul and his wife, Maggie, base their relationship on those three special little words—"diet starts Monday."

www.gotchacoveredfranchising.com

plinenberg@gotchacovered.com

720.407.8618

THE BEST OPPORTUNITY YOU'VE *NEVER* THOUGHT OF

By Paul Linenberg

We get it.

In fact, we have some fun with it.

We know that nobody grows up thinking that they want to sell custom window treatments for a living. That's exactly why we call ourselves "the best opportunity you've *never* thought of."

For the 99.99% of people who have never considered the custom window treatment industry as a profession, here is an experiment that might help you understand the market potential of custom window treatments:

The next time you leave your house, take a look at all the windows you see—homes, retail stores, restaurants, office buildings, condos, churches—the list goes on and on and on. All of those windows need some type of window treatment. Therein lies the opportunity that we have at Gotcha Covered!

Our franchise owners (with 100-plus locations across the U.S. and Canada) provide custom window treatments to residential and commercial clients through a hands-on consultative and informative process that has earned Gotcha Covered an astonishing reputation with our clients.

Our Reputation

One thing that separates Gotcha Covered from practically every other service company in any industry is our online reputation as expressed by our clients on Google, Facebook, and other review sites. Across all our locations, our average review score is an extraordinary 4.9 out of 5.0 stars!

As you can imagine, it is hard enough for *any* business, even those with just one location, to earn a 4.9-star reputation. To do it across so many locations and with thousands of reviews is something that we have yet to hear of in any other business! (By the way, if there is another company out there with a similar reputation, we'd love to hear about them.)

So, how did Gotcha Covered achieve such an amazing reputation?

Well, we attribute this reputation first and foremost to the caliber of our franchise owners. We are very selective in awarding franchises to those with a strong work ethic, a desire to succeed, an ability to follow a plan, and an aptitude for creating relationships.

Notice there are no specific career experiences on this list! Our franchise owners come from all walks of life, including teachers, homemakers, software engineers, sales professionals, accountants, managers, entrepreneurs, retail, HR, food services, journalism, real estate, health care, and many more, including military veterans like Cliff Oberg. Cliff has a story about success and perseverance that is worth telling.

Cliff's Story

Originally from a small town in Montana, Cliff joined the Air Force as a young man to see the world. Cliff spent 20 years in the Air Force before deciding to retire to civilian life. As he was preparing to leave the service, he explored his options for employment and business ownership, and ultimately decided that Gotcha Covered was a good fit for him—and we agreed!

Living in a warm climate had always been part of Cliff's dream, so when he left the service, he decided to start his business in Tampa, Florida. He had never lived there before and didn't know anybody who did. He had no contacts whatsoever.

Cliff went through the initial training class like everyone else does and started building his new business according to the Gotcha Covered recipe. Because he did not know anything about his territory, it took him some time simply to learn the lay of the land and figure out where the neighborhoods were, what businesses he could partner with, what marketing opportunities he had, and so on.

Because Cliff was starting from scratch, it took him longer than most to start gaining traction, booking appointments, and closing sales. He had good days and bad days, as all new business owners inevitably do. He leaned on the Gotcha Covered staff, stuck to the plan, and maintained a high level of activity.

Eventually, Cliff's efforts started to pay off. Big time. Just after completing his first full year in business, Cliff set a record within Gotcha Covered of being the owner to open up a retail showroom in the shortest amount of time! (Our business model allows our franchise owners complete flexibility as to the structure of their business, whether home-based or with a showroom, with employees or without—the choice is up to them.) Later that year, Cliff found himself on stage at our annual conference, being recognized as one of our top ten performing franchise owners.

As impressive as Cliff's story is, the most impressive point is about what happened after he had spent many years as a top ten performer. You see, eventually, Cliff grew tired of the warm climate and longed to move back to his hometown.

After putting his business up for sale, a fellow Gotcha Covered owner who lived about 30 miles away decided to buy Cliff's business, leaving Cliff a nice nest egg to move back to Montana and semi-retire. But Cliff didn't retire. He could have gotten a job. But Cliff didn't get a job. He could have opened a fly-fishing business. But Cliff didn't open up a fly-fishing business. Nope, Cliff could have done literally anything else upon moving back home, but what he decided to do was to start another Gotcha Covered business!

Cliff's story says so much about how anyone with a desire to succeed, a strong work ethic, and solid interpersonal skills can be successful within Gotcha Covered. It says so much about the ability to build a business that has value when it's time to move on. The fact that his Gotcha Covered neighbor bought his business says so much about the desirability of a Gotcha Covered franchise. And the fact that Cliff decided to open another Gotcha Covered business speaks for itself.

Training and Support

But of course, we did not achieve our incredible reputation simply by bringing good people like Cliff into our system.

Over many years, we have developed a world-class training and support infrastructure that is relentlessly franchisee centric. This means that everything we do from a training and support perspective is driven by a focus to help our franchise owners be successful.

Our training starts with a full week of in-person or virtual training around a variety of topics, including measuring, technology, operations, marketing, and sales. This week of training has been continuously fine-tuned and honed over the years and gives our owners the very best foundation for success. We also have a full second week of in-home training where our franchise owners focus on product knowledge directly from our vendor partners.

After the first two weeks of formal training, our owners focus on getting their infrastructure set up, building their marketing strategy, and generally getting everything in place to launch their business. Gotcha Covered staff provide a lot of support and handholding during this very exciting and busy phase. Once all the pieces are in place, it's time to go!

After the business is launched, our owners start having appointments and making sales, learning more about products and the business along the way. Within the next couple of months, and with some experience and context, our owners come back for our advanced training class.

This week includes a lot of dialogue with other new owners, along with subject matter experts presenting advanced topics. At the conclusion of advanced training, our owners have been accelerated through the learning curve and are able to turbocharge their businesses.

While our incredible reputation has mostly to do with our owners and our training and support resources, there are other aspects of the Gotcha Covered system that contribute to the love we feel from our clients. After all, you simply can't achieve excellence without "hitting on all cylinders," as they say. Our technology is one of those cylinders.

The Point of Technology

Technology for technology's sake is pointless. Unless technology improves or enhances the results for the user, there is literally no point in it. That is why Gotcha Covered invests heavily in performance-based technology that focuses on helping our owners do more with less and ultimately put more dollars in their pockets.

Gotcha Covered was actually founded as a technology company that developed a unique software program for our industry. Technology is still part of our DNA, and we have spent many years and many dollars creating a comprehensive web-based operational software, called Gotcha Linked, that is unlike any other software program in our industry.

Gotcha Linked is a full, front-end, lead management, marketing automation platform that helps our franchise owners manage prospects, calendars, pricing and proposals, tasks, projects and a whole lot more. Gotcha Linked provides advanced business intelligence and integration with QuickBooks, among other third-party software programs. At the end of the day, Gotcha Linked provides our franchise owners with efficiencies and tools that help them run all aspects of their business with a strong client focus.

Growing the Brand

Another important aspect of our online reputation is a robust and comprehensive data-driven marketing platform. Our multi-channel marketing strategies and tactics are based on sophisticated data and include proven offline and online marketing tools and resources. In particular, Gotcha Covered has several automated marketing programs that allow our franchise owners to focus on local engagement and lead generation. This collaborative marketing approach helps our owners find our best customers, build trust and credibility, and ultimately build ongoing revenue streams.

A Crystal Ball

So, what does the future of the custom window treatment industry look like?

The window treatment industry, generally speaking, is quite fragmented with little branding and lagging in technology. It is one of the few remaining industries that has not yet undergone significant consolidation.

As technology becomes a more critical aspect of our industry, and as marketing becomes increasingly complex, the smaller, independent "mom and pop" window treatment retailers will find it harder and harder to compete against a powerhouse like Gotcha Covered. They simply don't have the resources, the efficiencies, or the technological competence to keep up.

Gotcha Covered is in the perfect position to capitalize on the evolution of our industry. Our technology, our marketing savvy, and our amazing reputation are the perfect building blocks to ultimately become a dominant player in our industry. Having achieved the milestone of 100 locations in 2019, we are building momentum, accelerating our growth responsibly, and are well on our way to becoming a household name.

Qualified people who are ready to associate with a high-quality brand, find an optimal work/life balance, and create the income and equity that they desire should take a serious look at Gotcha Covered. We can't guarantee that we will be a good fit for everyone, but why not take a closer look at the best opportunity you've never thought of?

Chapter

Sixteen

An ActionCOACH For Every Business, Why It's Never Been A Better Time

Rick Moore

Rick Moore

ActionCOACH Canada

Rick Moore is the CEO of ActionCOACH Canada. He is well into his third decade of working with business owners to achieve their dreams and goals. He has financed and advised both public and private businesses.

He has co-founded two companies, worked in C-suite roles, sat on several boards, and worked as a coach and consultant.

During his 38 years in the Canadian business community, Rick has had the privilege of raising startup capital and advising many great businesses. In fact, two have reached the billion-dollar mark in value. His ability to see the potential in, and believe in, business owners are traits that form his purpose and allow for him to fulfill why he goes to work every day.

Coaching business owners is where Rick finds his passion. Each day he brings his strong belief that every business deserves to succeed. He now brings that passion for building the ActionCOACH Canada team of coaches throughout the country.

Rick is an author and public speaker. Populating Canada with the best trained and most inspired coaches is his mission.

www.actioncoachfranchise.ca

rick@actioncoach.ca

www.linkedin.com/in/rick-moore-4069383a/

Toll-free 1-800-700-3850

AN ACTIONCOACH FOR EVERY BUSINESS, WHY IT'S NEVER BEEN A BETTER TIME

By Rick Moore

The husband turned to his wife and said, "If that is all we can get for the business, we might just as well keep working." Those words and the dejected look on their faces changed my life then and there.

I had an epiphany, and though I did not know it at the moment, it led me to an industry that allows me to live my purpose each day. Let me explain.

After thirty-two years of assisting business owners to start up, raise capital, and advise them as they grew, I was now on the other side of the table, the buy-side. This is the point at which a business owner is ready to sell, to reap the rewards for all the years of hard work, long hours and the payback for taking the risk to be their own boss. If we purchased the business, those dreams would be fulfilled. The truth is that far too often, the scene above was playing out. Why? The reasons are many; however, suffice to say that a huge percentage of business owners have not set up their business to sell. A buyer looks for many things. They need the business to operate smoothly, grow and be profitable for them. Far too many businesses are missing key ingredients, and worse, they have an inflated sense of what the business is worth.

Back to that epiphany—I realized that day that this problem was solvable. I made a list of the most common "blind spots" I was encountering. I came up with several that I knew we could make work. When I say "we," I mean business coaches. Not consultants, trainers, or leadership coaches. Great business coaches exhibit the best of all of those. I mean, a coach that is there for you can guide you to implement great processes and hold you accountable. Every athlete has a coach; in fact, all the great business leaders of our time have them.

You are great at what you do, but nobody ever prepared you for the management and scaling that a business needs as it grows. A business coach does not need to know anything about plumbing or fashion design. They do know the basics that are the foundation of every business, no matter the industry.

Business coaching is the second-fastest-growing industry worldwide. When approached to lead ActionCOACH Canada, I jumped at the chance. Leading this team, I can exponentially grow the number of business owners that have access to our world-class coaching.

Starting your Business—the Critical Initial Steps

I worked in an industry for 32 years, where I met hundreds of business owners. Many at an early stage. In fact, at a stage so early, they were looking for someone who believed in them almost more so than the business plan. I raised capital and advised many businesses, some small, some large. Some succeeded, and some did not.

The difference between success and failure plays out in many ways. As said, there are blind spots that owners need to be on the lookout for. What you read from here on out is why business coaches are so in demand. Every blind spot and the stories I will tell all fall under the umbrella of how a business coach can make a significant difference in business outcomes

Blind Spots

Need

Too many businesses start, money is invested and spent, and, when launched, there is no interest. This is too late to realize the mistake. It was avoidable. The guidance and accountability of a coach will be the best initial investment you can make. This applies to any new business or any new product or service being added to an existing company. The need for the product or service must be perceived by the end-user to have value that they are willing to pay for. Any effort here needs to be tested and measured in a small way. If changes are needed, they can be made and tried again—the same process. Ultimately you find the right audience or the idea must be discontinued.

Systems

Simply put, systems must be in place; the systems run the business—the people operate the systems. This allows people to change with no slow down to business operations. Your coach will help you put systems in place. The systems operate the business; the employees operate the systems. You will be able to work on growing the business with the newfound surplus cash flow you are generating, not problem-solving and helping customers all day long.

Confusing Marketing and Sales

Marketing leads to sales; however, it is its own unique process. To have one person doing both jobs is not effective and efficient. Make sure you are driving enough people to your sales funnel. These leads are generated from your marketing efforts. Once you have a customer, marketing also is key in the customer returning again and again to purchase. Marketing must take many forms and should always be tested and measured, changed if not working, continued if it is.

Sales, the process and the ultimate sale, is the result of an excellent marketing strategy. Your sales process needs to have clear and concise steps. It must be tracked for success and delivered at world-class levels

Hiring

The key people in the right positions are critical. The hiring process is key here. Look at every employee and ask yourself, would I hire them again if I had to today? Do not take on any new employee until you have fully maximized the current staff, including managers who may have spare hours to assist.

Market-based wage

Many owners do not pay themselves a wage, or if they do, it is small. They rely on year-end profits to take a dividend. The profits may not be there to take a dividend. Not paying yourself a wage that you would have to pay a person to do what you do results in a flawed valuation and breakeven numbers. There is no sense fooling yourself. Until you take a salary that is the going rate, then your numbers are a lie.

Growth

Always be thinking of your growth. Are you growing fast? If so, make sure management of the growth is in place. Plan continued growth at least ten years out. Always be thinking about potential strategic buyers or partners that can use what you do to enhance their business? Ultimately when you want to sell, the purchaser needs to know the company can grow.

Owners Trap

This is where an owner must be on the job every day for the business to operate efficiently. Owners work long hours and have limited time off. Why? Your employees and customers rely on the owner for every contact or operational issue. This leaves no time for the owner to grow the business. It will also result in a lower valuation as the main asset is leaving the business when sold to a new owner.

Revenue/Cash Flow

Revenue is vanity. Growing revenue is only meaningful if it falls profitably to the bottom line. If it is tied up in working capital timelines, or spent on inefficient labor, then it is robbing the business of the oxygen it needs to grow. This dilemma plays out many times in business, Revenue that eats up cash when the gap between when you pay and when you get paid will suck the oxygen out of your business. You must keep your working capital timelines as short as possible. Your ActionCOACH will show you how to negotiate better payment and receivable terms and maximize your labor efficiency

Valuation

Owners believe they know the value of the business. They are often very wrong, as was the case at the beginning of this chapter. The result of these blind spots and many others is that many businesses do not sell, or if they do, not in a way that satisfies the seller. A survey conducted in 2017 by Mass Mutual discovered that about 50% of respondents said they had a valuation of their business done; however, one in four of those said they did it themselves. Remember, the buyer is at the starting line of the marathon; you are approaching the finish. They are looking for future growth, stable profits and systems that will allow them to seamlessly step in and operate your business.

I have always believed in business owners. Here are two short examples and the role that coaching did or did not play.

In 1995 a fellow showed up at my office. His passion was evident; he was someone worth backing. He was going to purchase one small insurance agency in his hometown of High River, Alberta. The current owners were retiring. He realized that throughout Western Canada, in small towns, this was the situation—long time owners were looking to retire. He wanted to acquire these agencies and build a rural network of insurance brokerages. His goal would be to add banking, life insurance and other financial services.

He grew and realized he no longer had the ability to manage the growth on his own. He sought out a coach, and with that in place, he turned a sleepy little insurance agency into a company that was sold for $440 million just 12 years after we launched it by raising $700,000. The company today does $1.5 billion in sales.

In 1999 two guys had an idea to turn a paper-intensive business into one managed with technology. The competition was some of the world's largest financial institutions. All of them still using paper. This was a bold initiative. They approached me and launched with a $2 million capital raise. They got great initial traction. Two world events then occurred that stymied their ability to raise further capital. Soon, one partner quit, leaving the other in the lurch. He gave it a valiant effort, but eventually, when money was found, the people with it wanted total control. He lost his company. With the proper capital and fully aligned management group, this company grew and sold for $1.2 billion to Morgan Stanley. The problems arose for the two original owners when they were not clearly aligned with the same vision. They expanded too rapidly and lacked the processes to scale back and wait out the storm. They hired for rapid growth, and the business struggled to make payroll. A coach from the very start could have identified every aspect of the problems that caused them to lose the company.

This chapter is about coaching. The need for coaches and the need for businesses to hire them. It is about ActionCOACH, the number one business coaching company in the world. For 27 years, in over 80 countries, we deliver results for 18,000 businesses every week.

The statistical battleground for business owners is daunting. We know 75% of all medium and small businesses in Canada are run by baby boomers. In the next decade, those businesses will be transitioning ownership. That represents $1.5 trillion of wealth transfer in Canada alone. The playing field as it stands is not level. Buyers have their choice. They will only pay for businesses that have all areas operating at maximum efficiency.

Note in the two successes the difference that coaching played in how the founders exited the business.

Hiring an ActionCOACH is an investment for which the business receives a return or "return on investment" (ROI).

The client success anchors the potential ROI on your investment in becoming a partner with us. The average ROI for our clients is impressive. We deliver great service and great outcomes.

We stand out, even in our peer group, as a unique, results-orientated firm. Our proven products and services work. They can be applied in any business, in any industry, no matter the size or geography. If you are looking for a career change, want to monetize your business experience and want to scale a firm in a vibrant industry, then I would love to chat with you.

Chapter *Seventeen*

9 Holes Of Golf That Changed The World

Jeff Oddo

Jeff Oddo

Go CityWide

In 1961, my father Frank launched City Wide Maintenance to provide Kansas City businesses quality janitorial services. Growing up in their family grocery stores, Frank saw just how hard it was to attract and retain good people to clean their stores at night. Knowing other business owners must struggle with the same thing, he decided to specialize in quality janitorial services you could count on. Frank's hunch paid off, and City Wide quickly grew to a leading provider in the area.

I, too, learned every aspect of our family businesses growing up. Starting in sales, then as General Manager, we grew the business 600% in six years. By 1997, I was heading up the company. With a new vision for our future, we transitioned City Wide's business model to a full-service facilities management company offering 20-plus services. This pivot created a unique opportunity for other entrepreneurs. So, in 2001, we launched City Wide Franchise, turning our thriving family business into a respected national brand.

I'm blessed to have worked with my family, and I am honored to share my experiences, helping others achieve their goals. I am passionate about developing people who believe in making a difference in the world, including the three amazing daughters I have raised with my wife, Karen.

I am always looking for talented team members and entrepreneurs. If you want to learn more about us, let's talk!

https://gocitywide.com/

joddo@gocitywide.com

https://www.linkedin.com/in/jeffoddo/

855-209-8970

9 HOLES OF GOLF THAT CHANGED THE WORLD

By Jeff Oddo

Hey, Jeff Oddo here, CEO and Owner of the City Wide Franchise Company. Welcome to my story. Now, I believe this is going to be the best chapter in the book, not just because it's the City Wide story. But because *this* is a story about how franchising (and some of the most amazing people I know) turned a successful 30-year-old company cleaning three million square feet a night into an international powerhouse brand managing over five hundred million today!

Just to preface, I've written this as historical fiction with a twist of satire. That means the following conversation took place, but my dad never called me these names. While he might not have been a believer in the model at first, he has always been a champion of me. I just chose to take a little creative license to make it, well, more amusing. So here we go.

In the early 2000s, I knew more about golf than franchising—and that's not saying much. To be frank, I had a dream, a great team at City Wide in Kansas City, and a whole lot of passion for making a difference in the world. But I also had a whole lot more questions than answers. For example, I didn't know anything about market size, competition, or the ideal candidate. And leadership and vision casting were just ideals. But boy, how things have changed in 19 years! Not only have many of those questions been answered, but my golf game (thankfully) took a back seat to the pursuit of something far better—franchising! And now, the only time I golf is to have some great (and humbling) discussions with my dad. At 84 years old, he can still beat me, while at the same time, challenging my ideas. He definitely keeps me on my toes.

Keep in mind, I love my dad. He is my greatest hero and mentor. He, my mother and my brothers have taught me so much, and I am blessed to be a member of the family. Here is how he "helped me" with City Wide Franchise. I call it "The Nine Holes of Golf That Changed the World."

Hole One

Jeff: Hey, Dad, I am thinking about starting a franchise company. Want to hear about it?

Dad: Nope!

Hole Two

Jeff: Come on, Dad. This is a great idea. I want to franchise City Wide.

Dad: You're an idiot. No one will ever pay you money to be a janitor.

Jeff: Dad! We aren't janitors anymore. You know this!

Dad: So, you've said. Now, shut up and hit the ball. People are waiting for you already.

Hole Three

Jeff: So, about this franchising idea—

Dad: Can we talk about something else? Haven't we beat that franchising thing to death on the previous two holes? It's not going to work.

Jeff: Seriously? How old are you anyway? Are you getting senile on me already? You told me I was an idiot and it wouldn't work. That's been our entire discussion on the subject. I hardly think that's beating it to death. So, no, we can't talk about something else yet. This is a great idea, Dad!

Dad: Alright, alright! Go ahead but make it quick. We have lots of other things to talk about today—like maybe your terrible swing!

Jeff: Dad, just think about the possibilities. Heck, had you not started City Wide Maintenance in 1961, this wouldn't even be possible! I guess that time in the Air Force actually did you some good because we know that worthless business degree from Missouri University didn't do you any good. Too bad you weren't smart enough to go to Kansas State like me!

Dad: Ha! Real men go to MU! You're just mad they wouldn't accept you, and K-State had no choice.

Jeff: Seriously, I think it's pretty cool that you got your idea while working for your dad, and I got my idea for franchising while working for you. Pretty cool, huh?

Dad: Remember, you don't work *for* me, dummy, you work *with* me. And there's a big difference between our ideas. I knew how hard it was to attract and retain good people to clean our stores at night. So, if we were struggling with that issue, I knew other business owners would be as well. My idea was great, and your idea is stupid!

Jeff: Ha, you are a funny guy! Funny looking, too! Yeah, you got lucky—for once. Every 60 years, I guess you deserve a break!

Hole Four

Jeff: But Dad, you really need to understand this franchising thing. We are *not* a cleaning company anymore. When we moved to independent contractors and part-time facility managers, we expanded our focus on basic janitorial services to becoming a world-class sales organization that provides more than 20 different facilities management solutions. That's a real difference maker! That change in our business model gave City Wide something unique to franchise.

Hole Five

Dad: You are so busy. Why in the world would you want to take on another project like this?

Jeff: Because it's important for the future. You know how I have been in that CEO group for the last ten years or so? The one where we act as each other's outside board of directors and have amazing speakers?

Dad: Do I know? Are you kidding me? That CEO group costs us a fortune!?! Don't forget, I am a Depression baby! I remember when mom and I would allocate 15 cents a day for meals, and we thought if we made $1,000 a week from the business, we would be rich. All we had back then was each other, our smarts, and a lot of hard work.

Jeff: Well, we also don't walk to school anymore—uphill—both ways—in six feet of snow. And bread is not a nickel either, Pops. Times change. And this Vistage group is one of the best things I've experienced in my career. I've learned so much from others and met some really interesting people, one of which was Tom Hill, coauthor of *Chicken Soup for the Soul*. He challenged us to think differently about business. That there was more to life than just making money and being financially successful. He said in order to be completely fulfilled, you have to become significant. And the best way to do that was to franchise your business and teach others what has made you successful. That's why I want to franchise! I want to give back. I want to help others accomplish what we have accomplished. I am a middle child, a pleaser, a giver. I want people to be in control of their lives and happy with what they do.

Dad: If you want people to be happy, let's start with golf lessons. Your game is making me cry. Is that a double bogie or triple?

Hole Six

Dad: Okay, let's suppose for a second that you do franchise this concept, is there a market for it?

Jeff: According to Fredenious Group and ISSA, the facilities industry is a $100 billion dollar industry. In fact, it's one of the largest industries out there, not to mention it is almost recession-proof, constantly growing, has recurring revenue. In our model, we won't have any equipment, inventory or probably even hourly employees. The best part about the industry is it an *essential* industry!

Hole Seven

Dad: Ok, so you've done your homework. What's *your* vision? What do *you* think you can accomplish?

Jeff: I want us to be the first choice! I want City Wide to be special for many reasons. But one of the most important ones will be because of our *vision* of being the first choice—for franchise owners, employees, clients, independent contractors and vendors in every market we serve. I want our community members to feel like there is no one else they would rather work for, do business with, or be in a business relationship with than City Wide.

Dad: Sounds like what a lot of other companies say. How do *you* plan on doing it?

Jeff: It won't be easy. I know that if we want to be a billion-dollar brand, a top 100 concept and to be the fastest-growing, most successful management company in the building maintenance industry, we will have to be great at attracting and retaining people who embrace our purpose and understand that from a client's perspective, *what makes us unique* is that we provide part-time facility managers who represent their needs rather than the service companies who provide the work.

Hole Eight

Dad: Ok, where does all that Siegfried and Roy stuff you keep telling me about fit into this?

Jeff: Dad, it's not Siegfried and Roy; it's Maslow. But right now, you mean Simon Sinek. He talks about the why and the purpose. I want a company whose mission is truly focused on positively impacting as many people in our communities as possible. I want our *purpose* to be our people! And while I might not even know most of the people that work for our contractors or franchisees personally, I want each and every one of them to know they are a valuable member of the City Wide team and they truly matter to our business. I have always felt it is a sincere honor and privilege to lead our team in Kansas City with their professional careers. So, we will surround ourselves with people who feel the same way all across the country! And maybe even the world!

Dad: World domination now?

Jeff: I'm thinking big here. To make people our purpose, we will need people who share our core values of community, accountability, and professionalism. People who embrace having God as the foundation for all we do, so we can give thanks. And we will definitely want to empower them to make decisions based upon the Golden Rule.

Dad: Never lend money to your brothers?

Jeff: No, the other Golden Rule—treating people the way they would want to be treated. And that, my dear Dad, was par.

Hole Nine

Dad: You need to stop reading all these books and get outside more often. You are starting to actually make sense! Who is your competition?

Jeff: That's the great part! We don't really have any. We will eventually, but not now. Sure, there are hundreds of companies that do the work; people who do the cleaning, the grass cutting, the painting, and security, but I am not aware of anyone who provides part-time facility managers who are paid to save clients time and solve their facility challenges.

Dad: Alright, I'll consider it. You're buying lunch, though, since you talked my ear off.

It was a hard sell, trust me. But we launched City Wide Franchise in 2001. And as of 2021, City Wide has over 70 locations in the U.S. and Canada, serving more than 11,000 clients and positively impacting the lives of more than 21,000 thousand families.

We look for franchise owners who resonate with our story and leaders who give and get respect. We want winners who love their teams, are fun to be around, believe in continuous learning, and are hungry to make a difference in this world.

Although other great franchise companies exist, *no one* can imitate the soul, the passion, and the commitment of our owners and our teams. Our amazing business model, support system, and everything needed to build a healthy business are only as great as the people in it. People are truly our purpose! And they are what make City Wide a powerhouse brand!

I tell all our community members I want City Wide to be their home for a long time. I want them to be able to say City Wide is the best organization they have *ever* worked for/with. More importantly, I pray that "spreading the ripple" to make a difference is more than just a saying. I pray it is the number one driver that gets them energized to come to work each and every day!

Caring about others is contagious, so ripple on!

Chapter

Eighteen

Outsourced Financial Support For Small Business Owners

Jeff Provost

Jeff Provost

SmartBooks

Jeff Provost is the Chief Operating Officer with SmartBooks, where he leads the organization in providing outsourced bookkeeping, accounting, and finance services to franchises and small businesses. Jeff has worked in many types of businesses, from start-up to Fortune 100 companies, and he especially loves working directly with small business owners to improve their operations and utilize their financial data and operational metrics to make smart business decisions. As of this writing, Jeff is working towards his

Certified Franchise Executive (CFE) certification through the International Franchise Association and is an active participant in the franchise community both as a franchise supplier and a franchisor.

Contact Information:

www.smartbooks.com

jprovost@smartbooks.com

www.linkedin.com/in/jeffreyprovost

978-905-6346

OUTSOURCED FINANCIAL SUPPORT FOR SMALL BUSINESS OWNERS

By Jeff Provost

The Industry

According to the U.S. Small Business Administration, there are approximately 31 million small businesses in the United States, with fewer than 20 employees, and hundreds of thousands of new businesses are started each year.

How many people go into business for themselves and enthusiastically say: "I want to do my own books and spend time managing my business finances"?

Or even better, how many actually know how to interpret financial data and use that information to make decisions that can help them improve the overall performance of the business?

Many people go into business for themselves to do what they love, or at least to build something for themselves instead of someone else. They want to be in control; they want to live the lifestyle of their choosing and produce income that supports their hopes and dreams.

Sadly, many business owners don't know how their business is *actually* performing, and if it's not helping them achieve their financial goals, they lack the financial acumen and resources to improve their business performance.

Every small business could benefit from a CFO. Not every business can afford a CFO. Or maybe they can.

My Story

Back in 2010, I was working at the Staples corporate office in Framingham, Massachusetts. I had been there for about seven years and, by all accounts, had a great thing going—multiple promotions up the corporate ladder, making good money, and working for an established brand that was admired and respected by many. However, something was missing. Despite my relative success, I felt a conflict between the work that I was doing and the lack of connection to an overall purpose that I believed in. Although Staples was, and still is, an amazing company, I grew tired of the big public company world and all of the red tape and bureaucracy that comes with it, and felt the need to do something different.

When I told my family that I was leaving Staples to join a technology startup, they thought I was crazy, and I didn't disagree. But I believed that there was more to work and life than what I was doing. I was tired of having a separate "work persona" that was oftentimes in conflict with how I lived my life outside of work. So, I took a leap of faith, left my "secure" corporate job and went into the technology startup world.

Ten years and four companies later, I do not have a single regret. All of the leaps of faith I have taken along the way, and all of the mistakes I have made and setbacks I have experienced, have prepared me to do the work that I do in my role as the Chief Operating Officer at SmartBooks.

I joined SmartBooks in 2018, nine years after the company was founded by husband and wife Calvin and Jenny Wilder. Cal and Jenny started the business with a simple conviction:

"Small business owners deserve better." Better understanding of their financial performance. Better access to resources that are typically only available to medium and large-sized businesses. Better use of their own time to do the work that they truly enjoy doing—which usually is not managing their financials and other back-office duties.

When Cal hired me in 2018, the thing that most endeared me to Cal and to SmartBooks was the overarching purpose of helping small business owners. There was such a strong vision of what SmartBooks could become and a history of growth and success that already existed, and I found it contagious. But how can we go from a regional player supporting 150 clients to a national player supporting thousands of small businesses? Time and again, Cal has reminded our team that the company is SmartBooks—not Wilder and Wilder—and we want to build a business and a brand that is bigger than any of us. But how?

SmartBooks Service Offering

For 11 years, SmartBooks has been providing outsourced bookkeeping, accounting, finance, payroll, HR, and tax services to small businesses.

Our services are grounded in a few core beliefs:

Small businesses need more than bookkeeping. While clean books are a must-have for small businesses, owners need much more financial support to make key decisions to keep their business thriving.

Small business owners deserve access to experts at a price they can afford. With SmartBooks' team-based approach, small business owners have access to experienced

CFOs, CPAs, certified HR and payroll specialists, all for a fraction of the cost of a single full-time generalist.

Small businesses can—and should—get more for their dollar. Service packages and an operational model designed specifically for small businesses change the economics of service delivery, giving business owners and executives a high-quality service they can count on without breaking any budgets.

Small business owners shouldn't have to settle. Most small businesses are stuck choosing between a part-time specialist who's rarely available or a full-timer who may be great in a thousand different ways but simply isn't a trained bookkeeper or accountant. SmartBooks changes that.

Many small business owners reach out to SmartBooks because they want help getting their books in order. Perhaps they have been doing it on their own and recognize that their time is better spent on other activities. Perhaps their spouse is handling the books and tells the owner that if they don't find another option then—well, who knows what comes after then, but they feel compelled to find a better solution. Perhaps the bookkeeper they have been with for a while is moving on. Perhaps they just know that they're not getting good quality from their current provider, but they can't articulate what good looks like.

Regardless of what their current solution entails, the common theme is that they come to SmartBooks looking for a better bookkeeping solution—they know what they want. In almost every case, as we delve into their business model and ask them questions about what they will do once they have a solid foundation in place with their books, the conversation turns to more strategic financial questions and issues:

How should I think about investing in sales and marketing?

I want to sell my business in five years. What should I start planning for now?

How can I understand which of my clients or projects are most/least profitable?

What are the metrics and scorecards that I should put in place to help me get on track to achieving my long-term goals?

With the SmartBooks service offering, we can engage at the most basic level with a small business owner—bookkeeping. We can get their books cleaned up, implement a proper chart of accounts that is aligned with their industry and business model, keep up with the regular coding and categorization of transactions, and provide monthly bank and credit card reconciliations so they can get more insight into their business' performance. Once the basics are in place, and they have confidence that they are being done well and consistently, we can add more value to the relationship. Perhaps we can start by building a budget and forecast and then doing monthly budget versus actual reporting. Or maybe they are in a cash crunch, and we can do cash flow analysis and 13-week cash flow projections. No matter where they are in their journey, we can add value.

In 2020, Cal wrote and published a book titled, *The Financial Operating System: Empowering Small Business Owners To Take Control Of Their Finances and Improve Their Financial Fitness* (available on Amazon). This book is a culmination of the many years of experience that Cal has as both a fractional CFO for hundreds of small businesses, as well as founding and running several businesses of his own.

The Financial Operating System® codifies the way in which we approach client engagements at SmartBooks. Business owners who work with SmartBooks have consistent and reliable financial data that they can rely on to make smarter business decisions and a team of experts that can handle the routine tasks well while also providing them strategic guidance and support. We have helped countless business owners sell their business, scale and raise capital, or just achieve the levels of revenue and profitability they desire that enable them to live the lifestyle they want. No matter the goal, small business owners have more confidence when there is a team standing alongside them that will be there to support them. And when they hire SmartBooks, they have more time to work *on* their business instead of getting bogged down *in* their business.

How SmartBooks Got Involved in Franchising

In 2019 I was introduced to the franchise world through someone who has become a friend and colleague, Chris Meibers. I was showing Chris the Genie software application that our sister company was developing and how that application, coupled with our core service offering, could help small business owners. Chris has extensive experience in franchising and introduced us to an emerging brand, which became our first franchise system client. Since then, we have continued to gain traction by working directly with franchisees to provide outsourced bookkeeping, accounting and finance support as they work towards opening their business and scaling with them as they grow. I have continued immersing myself in the franchise world—building relationships, pursuing my Certified Franchise Executive (CFE) designation, and learning as much as I can about the franchise business model and industry.

At the IFA 2020 conference, Cal and I were brainstorming growth ideas, and the topic of franchising SmartBooks came up. This was something that Cal had considered previously, and after seeing the success we were starting to have as a franchise supplier, the idea began to get some traction.

Franchise Opportunity

SmartBooks began offering franchise licenses in 2021. SmartBooks has a strong and memorable brand, a team of experts to support our Franchisees, a robust system of tools and processes based on 11 years of experience, and a target small business owner end-customer that needs our support more than ever.

What makes a successful franchisee?

Do you have experience working as CFO, Vice President of Finance, Director of Finance, or another similar role with financial planning and analysis and management responsibility for a business or non-profit organization?

Are you looking to build a business of your own, doing the work you love, that has enterprise value beyond your billable hours? Do you love helping business owners get a better handle on their finances?

This may be your time to consider investing in a SmartBooks Franchise.

Our purpose at SmartBooks is to empower healthy business. We believe a healthy business must have strong financial management, which then carries over into all aspects of the business to fuel results. The SmartBooks franchise opportunity enables you to build a healthy business of your own while supporting small business owners in your market to run a healthy business.

What you get when you invest with SmartBooks:

A home-based business and an established and scalable recurring revenue business model

Access to our recommended small business technology stack for small business finance support

Ability to serve as a fractional CFO/strategic business advisor to small business owners, while also supporting them with quality bookkeeping and accounting services

Training on a variety of aspects of the SmartBooks Way, including generating new business opportunities, closing new sales contracts, and servicing and retaining clients.

Access to The Financial Operating System®, including training on how to conduct The Financial Operating System® Bootcamps and implementing and using The Financial Operating System® for clients.

Access to an online resource center containing a robust operations manual that outlines all aspects of how to run your franchise business and support from your Franchise Support Team as challenges arise.

A franchisor that truly believes we are not successful unless you are successful.

Fractional CFO Business Owners Wanted

We are actively seeking applicants who have the background and desire outlined to become a Fractional CFO supporting small business owners. For more information, please visit www.smartbooks.com/franchise.

Chapter *Nineteen*

Goodbye Graffitti

Laurie Spivack

Laurie Spivack

Goodbye Graffiti

Laurie was born and grew up in NW Detroit and attended public school. Graduating from Michigan State University with a BA in independent studies and a focus on dance, she moved to New York City. She spent the next eight years performing, choreographing, and teaching. Her career highlights were a European teaching tour, contracts to choreograph for professional dance companies in the U.S.

and throwing out the first baseball at a Mets game disguised as Mickey Mouse.

Moving to Seattle, she continued her career successfully. Love changed that. She got married, had children and became a businesswoman. She started a business with her husband, bought real estate and opened a Goodbye Graffiti as a licensee to the Canadian franchisor.

Now, 18-plus years later, she has a 1+MM business and is the U.S. franchisor for Goodbye Graffiti.

Goodbye Graffiti USA

https//goodbyegraffitiusa.com

Laurie@goodbyegraffitiusa.com

Facebook/goodbyegraffitiusa.com

Instagram.com/goodbyegraffitiusa

LinkedIn.com/lauriespivack

(844) 648-1414

GOODBYE GRAFFITI

By Laurie Spivack

The drive for self-expression is part of the human condition. Self-expression unites us and divides us. We would not have art without it, fashion, government or even the frustrated tantrums of two-year-olds. But today, you will not see this need more graphically played out on our streets than in the prevalence of graffiti vandalism. Freeway overpasses, buildings, monuments, and any other available surfaces are up for grabs in the tagger's mind. So, what is graffiti?

Graffiti is not new, and it's been around longer than you may think. Archeologists around the world have uncovered countless examples of it. Newcastle University, February 27, 2019: Ancient graffiti has been found in a quarry near Hadrian's Wall in Carlyle, England. The graffiti depicts an officer and an image of a penis dating back to approximately 207 AD.

Merriam Webster defines graffiti as "usually unauthorized writing or drawing on a public surface." The operative word here is "unauthorized," or without permission.

In the U.S., it is not only unacceptable, but in most places, it is illegal to tag public and private property. Most large cities and many small cities around the country have ordinances on the books that make it illegal to tag and illegal to allow graffiti to dwell on property.

This creates an opportunity for a graffiti mitigation industry. Oh, and did I mention that graffiti vandalism is a generational issue that will *never* go away? This fact seals the deal. So, who removes graffiti? Let's take a look at some large U.S. cities. The following information was gleaned from Google searches of Yellow Pages, Yelp, and other sources.

Pittsburgh has no graffiti removal pros.

San Diego has janitors who will *also* remove graffiti.

Atlanta has pressure-washing companies that will *also* remove graffiti.

This small smattering of Google searches illustrates that there are few if any, professional graffiti removal services.

Okay, so we see the opportunity, but is there a market? How does $10-plus billion per year in the U.S. sound? Yes, public and private entities spend almost 11 billion dollars per year in the U.S![1]

Projecting any increase in dollars spent removing graffiti depend on a number of factors:

Employment statistics. When unemployment increases, so does the incidence of graffiti.

Population and density. Higher population and increase in density in an area are factors that increase the incidence of graffiti.

City ordinances that are enforced. Enforcement lowers the incidence of graffiti.

Season. Summer sees the most graffiti. Youth have more time on their hands. But don't write off winter. The cloak of

---

[1] Maia Research, 2019

darkness is a powerful lure to taggers wanting respect and recognition from their peers.

These factors can increase or decrease the incidence of graffiti in any given area. However, if sales projections in the coatings industry are also an indication of growth in the graffiti removal industry, then we can look forward to a 35% increase from 2020-2027. [2]

Goodbye Graffiti began with a man and the condominium where he lived in Vancouver, British Columbia, Canada. In 1997, his building got vandalized by graffiti tagging. He went to the condo board and asked if they would pay to have it removed. When they said yes, the idea was born. Perri Domm bought a truck, a pressure washer, and some off-the-shelf removal products. This was the birth of Goodbye Graffiti™.

His business grew quickly due to the need and his innovation. He had a line of proprietary removal products and anti-graffiti coatings created. He had proprietary software created and added recurring revenue streams to his business model. He designed custom canopies to house the equipment used to remove graffiti. And he began franchising.

At that time, as mentioned above, there were no businesses that offered graffiti removal as a specialized service, just pressure washers as an add-on service. Additionally, Perri knew enough about wall surfaces to know that just putting a pressure washer to the wall would most likely damage the wall. Unfortunately, this was the standard at the time. The

---

[2] Precedenceresearch.com

City of Vancouver had an anti-graffiti ordinance but, like most cities, had no services to offer taxpayers. So, the threat of being fined for graffiti on your building and few good resources to remove it, let alone removing it completely and without damage, created a void in the market. This was not particular to Canada. In the US, the same was true. Many cities had (and have increased over time) ordinances to remove graffiti from private property, but there were no professionals out there to get the job done—until we came along.

As our name Goodbye Graffiti™ implies, we are graffiti removal specialists. We remove graffiti off of anything from walls to statues to buoys (that's right, buoys). We guarantee our customers 100% removal with 0% damage. We can do this because we are graffiti removal specialists. We service businesses, and our primary customers are property managers. What we do for them is to make them heroes to their clients by solving the problem quickly and completely. We implement our service on a one-off basis and through our successful Ever-Clean™ program. This program provides our franchisees with monthly recurring revenue, the holy grail of successful business models.

We have removed over ten million pieces of graffiti since inception. We do it in a way that fills the market void and solves our customers' problems.

The road to becoming a Goodbye Graffiti franchisee is similar to other franchise concepts. Before anyone signs on the dotted line, there are tangibles and intangibles that must be determined and agreed upon in order to ensure the best opportunity for success.

Tangibles

Do you have the funds necessary for a successful foundation and launch?

Do you have the ability to work your new business full time?

Do you have space (whether at home or a rented shop/office space) to function properly?

Intangibles

Do you "get" the opportunity?

Do you have the competencies to become a successful business owner?

Do yours and Goodbye Graffiti's values and business cultures align?

Do you have the ability and desire to learn and follow our proven systems?

Are you the type of communicator who can motivate your team and inspire trust with your customers?

Are you interested in exploring business ownership as a Goodbye Graffiti franchisee? You will be provided with materials and conversations with us that will answer your initial questions. You will have the opportunity to speak with other Goodbye Graffiti franchisees who will give you the "low down" on life as a "GG zee." You will be provided a Zorakle assessment to take. This informative and enlightening assessment will help us determine how the intangibles match/align with the type of individual we are looking for. This individual, we feel, has what it takes to be successful with us. Of course, you will receive and study the Franchise Disclosure Document (FDD) and Franchise

Agreement (FA). We recommend that you take this to a franchise attorney for review. With everything else a go, you will be invited to our flagship operation in Seattle, Washington, to see how we do it. Spend a day with us, speak with our team, and go out in the field with our crews to get a feel for it.

Of course, you want to know what we provide to support your growth and success. Well, we've got lots!

How will you keep track of the hundreds of customers and properties you will be servicing? We have software for that. How will you archive the details of every building and asset you bid on and service? We have software for that. How will you create proposals and manage the sales process? We have software for that. How will you manage your fleet of vehicles and team of technicians? We have software for that too! Are you a numbers person who likes to identify and keep track of key performance indicators (KPIs)? Got you covered.

Our software programs, called Click-Off™ and Grafflinx™, are proprietary. They are designed to manage your data, follow the sales process, manage operations, track weekly sales, manage administration, and create monthly goals.

You will have exclusive access to our line of proprietary removal products, anti-graffiti coatings and methodologies that will allow you to give your customers 100% removal guarantees with 0% damage to their properties.

Not sure how to start a business? Our first manual will walk you through the process, provide resources, checklists and templates to help you get started.

Where does anyone learn to remove graffiti beside the back of a squirt bottle? Graffiti University, that's where. Our robust training program provides the ability to learn hands-on technical skills at our flagship Seattle location. You will be learning from our team with 20 years of collected knowledge and experience. We've seen it all, from graffiti on buildings, signs, vehicles, statuary, playground equipment, skate parks, even hedges. You will learn the best environmental and safety practices in order to keep you, the public and the environment safe and impact-free. Chemistry, equipment handling, shop operations and more.

Besides the extensive technical training, you will become fluent with our Click-Off™ and Grafflinx™ software, field sales and administration. Goodbye Graffiti USA also has a quick start marketing program called Initiate Launch. This customized program will get you in front of your market's stakeholders and leaders to begin to develop valuable relationships. These relationships can help secure work, now and in the future, as well as impress your stature as an expert in the field.

Once you have a working knowledge, it's back to your market to get started. But our training and support don't stop there. We will come to *your* market to help you fine-tune your skills and put you on the road to success.

It is your choice whether you want to start in a commercial or industrial space, but you don't have to. Do you have office and shop space at home? You can start your business there! You will build expansion into your plan and, as you grow, move to the next level when the time is right.

What about buy-in? Here are some details.

Franchise Fee: $45,000 (25% discount for veterans, first responders and their spouses)

Start-Up Kit: $7,000 in removal products, marketing materials, branded wear

Vehicle, canopy, decals, equipment, office, shop, business start-up expenses: $20,000-135,000 (Will you be financing your equipment or buying it outright?)

When I opened my Seattle operation in 2003, my main focus was sales. My team was me and Darren, my technician. Every evening after our kids went to bed, I did the administration for the biz as well as our other family business (a house painting business), which my husband ran. We quickly coined a family motto that described our two-family businesses: he puts it on, and I take it off. It seemed to work.

One of the things I've always loved about sales is that you develop relationships, whether long or short, and you never know where they can take you. This is where a story I love to share starts.

In our second year of business, I was out in the field looking for graffiti, and I found some on the home office of a large insurance company. The building was very large, and there was a lot of graffiti. I approached the security at the entrance and asked to speak with the facilities manager. I was handed the phone where the guy on the other end of the line said I could drop off or send some company info. Now I don't like hearing that because it slows the sales process. But I understood that this is how some organizations work.

I sent some materials in the mail and was called back a week or so later. We ended up cleaning all the graffiti and signed them up for our Ever-Clean™ weekly maintenance program. That was great!

Fast forward two years. The man I'd spoken with originally, whose name is John, moved from that organization to a regional transit authority as their facilities director, a decision-maker. He had me called out to discuss graffiti at one of their stations. We walked and talked, and the outcome was another Ever-Clean™ weekly maintenance program.

To my surprise, a couple months later, I received a request for proposal from them. They wanted this same program on 22 other stations! They used the structure of our program to create the scope of the program they wanted to create! Needless to say, we got the contract. It set us on a growth trajectory in a way that no other contract so far had.

We've worked that contract for ten years, and it's grown to 40 locations, earning over a million. But my story doesn't end there. Oh yes, my friend, there is more. Fast forward again to the summer of 2020. Social unrest across the nation, resulting in passionate protests and demands for justice. One by-product of this anger and frustration was graffiti vandalism. Neither public nor private property was spared. Along came my friend and associate, John, who now directs the fleets and facilities for the City of Seattle.

We set up daily patrols of five to eight city buildings, including police precincts, City Hall, and others. It felt like the summer of the hamster wheel. However, we earned thousands of dollars, maintained graffiti-free zones at these properties, and reestablished a loyal working relationship with our friend and associate, John.

During our conversations throughout the summer, John reiterated his desire to continue to work with us because of our dependability, fair pricing, quality work and great working relationship. What more could you want?

When my kids were kids, and I did something for them that they liked, I'd say to them, "This is the part where you say Thanks, Mom, you're the best!" So, this is the part where you say, "Wow, Laurie, I really see myself owning a Goodbye Graffiti USA franchise. What are the next steps?" I'm so glad you asked!

I see that you *see* the opportunity here and are prepared for a serious look at a business in a niche market that, otherwise, is quite void of talent and solutions. The numbers look good, and your mind is racing with possibilities.

That's fantastic! Contact us at:

844-648-1414

laurie@goodbyegraffitiusa.com

Chapter

Twenty

Building Relationships That Last A Lifetime

Scott Talley

Scott Talley

Network in Action

Scott Talley is a fourth-generation Houstonian. This "terminal entrepreneur" has started or purchased thirteen businesses in the last thirty years and, as he likes to say, "Some were winners and the others were teachers!" Proud father of three beautiful daughters: Danielle, 19, Sofia, 11, Alexa, 10, and at 58, he finally got his man JeanCarlo, now 6. He has been married to Moriah Talley for 12 years. Scott is the founder of Network In Action, a rapidly growing, industry-changing franchise that helps business owners and decision-makers, "Build relationships that last a lifetime." He is an avid golfer who loves to teach the game and its lessons to juniors of all ages.

https://www.networkinaction.com/

https://www.franchise.networkinaction.com/

scott@networkinaction.com

(857) 228-4669

BUILDING RELATIONSHIPS THAT LAST A LIFETIME

By Scott Talley

In the fall of 2013, I was 57 years old, and I had experienced both the thrill of business victory as well as the agony of defeat. Long gone were the days of a very successful publishing business that grew overnight to a 10-million-dollar entity. We were producing yellow pages for Better Business Bureaus with a business called "Consumer Guide." Consumer Guide had been recognized as one of the fastest growing businesses in the fifth largest city in the United States. In addition to printing directories, we were printing money.

We were flying high with over 60 salespeople around the country, and hard to believe, but our profits had grown for 13 straight years. Things were going so well we turned down an acquisition offer of $18 million!

In 2012 print advertising was a 26-billion-dollar industry, and over the next few years, only half of that! Over 400 publications failed nationwide in 12 months! When friends inquire about becoming print publishers, I remind them that if John Kennedy could not keep *George* magazine afloat, then what makes them think that they can!

As customers began to pull back on print advertising, I constantly worried about our reps and their families. Needless to say, there is no way anyone could really have predicted this, and I sure did not. There was a disaster in the making, and honestly, I failed as a leader. The crash was more like the Hindenburg than a soft landing.

I often say I am a terminal entrepreneur. Which translated means "no one will hire you, and you better learn to eat what you kill!" I have never been short on ideas, so fast forward a few years, and I had rebounded with a concept that I thought I was going to set the world on fire. It was called "OurBlok," and the idea was to connect hyper-local businesses with consumers in their own backyard. Think of a combined Facebook/LinkedIn group with a reward program where all the merchants were willing to give back to a local charity or group of your choice. We had spent thousands and thousands of dollars with this brilliant software that could be installed on any business's server, and within an hour or two, every merchant in the area could enjoy a rewards program and give back at the same time! The research showed that almost 65% of consumers would prefer to shop at a business that supported their causes!

One of the driving forces of my entrepreneurial journey has always been to give something back to the communities we serve. This particular software is fascinating. We could tie a consumer's phone number to the technology and allow them to choose a charity they like.

The concept was great, and in fact, we were enrolling businesses daily. Once the software is installed, a soccer mom who wanted to go and support her soccer team can order her pizza, use her phone number, and she not only would earn a reward, but the business would also contribute back to her favorite youth soccer team. There's only one problem, sometimes when you take a concept to market, the market is not ready.! We beat our heads against the wall for three years, trying to show businesses that the study showed all of these people would rather support a business giving back to their favorite charity. Well, that may be true in a study, but when someone offers a cheaper pizza, that goes out the window!

OurBlok was my first foray into franchising. After investing in the franchise documents and manuals, we awarded 14 OurBlok franchises in three years. The only problem was the customers were leaving us as fast as we could sign them up. To put it bluntly, our retention sucked, and life felt much like "the proverbial hamster on a treadmill." I was hell-bent on taking care of my franchise owners, and luckily, we were able to shut this entity down with everyone being made whole. The way I look at it, I spent three years and got a real education in franchising.

Now, at 57 years old with three daughters aged thirteen, four, and three, I did what millions of others have done. I looked for an industry with some upside and no barriers to entry. Plopped down my last $2,000 to my name and put my wife and me in real estate school. I was miserable. I love real estate but hated the fact that straight out of the training, I had to deal with veteran real estate agents who were hopeless.

I remember the night like it was yesterday. I told my wife that since I still owned the OurBlok in our neighborhood that she should put her pretty little white pearls on, and I would take pictures of her and market the heck out of her real estate business. I followed that up with, "It won't do any good. You need a networking group."

I had many years of experience with traditional networking groups. Getting together every week in the early mornings with powdered eggs and overcooked bacon! Small talk, bad jokes, and a ton of wasted time. These groups were typically run by volunteers; they were full of people trying to sell me something. Some of those volunteers were great leaders, but just as often, you would get someone who had little knowledge of leadership and no desire to follow the approved plan. The day you joined, you were required to start bringing your friends so they too could participate in the insanity!

I had even called the leader of the biggest networking group in the country to find out about starting a group. I remember asking how would we be compensated? I was told that I could spend my time going out and recruiting businesspeople, and then I would have the benefit of one year on the house! Let's see, I could donate countless hours, send in weekly reports, deal with petty politics, all for a stipend of $500 a year!

Shortly after that conversation and by the grace of God, I picked up an iPad and decided to do some research. It was about 10:00 p.m., the family was asleep when I simply Googled "reviews of networking groups." I came across a thread, and after about 45 minutes of reading, I grabbed a tablet and pen and continued to read for another two hours taking notes on themes that seemed to run throughout this research. When I finished, it was 1:00 am. my sleepy wife woke and inquired, "What in the world have you been doing?" I immediately responded, "I have the greatest idea I've ever had."

The next morning, I could not wait to get to the office even though it had been a very depressing place for a long time. Somehow, I had hung onto my right-hand man, a great IT guy named Danielo Rojas. I begin to explain to Danielo that I felt like there was a void in the market that we could fill. As I tried to explain, it was something between traditional networking and LinkedIn. He responded, “Sorry boss, that already exists, and it’s called Meetup.” I remember initially having the wind taken out of my sails. I explained that in my humble opinion, the world needs a place for business owners and decision-makers who are busy and want to build meaningful relationships.

With that, the birth of Network In Action Franchise International. In the fourth quarter of 2013, I started to have discussions with business owners about an entirely new concept. I had no idea if this was going to work, but I knew that I had a family to feed, and no one was going to hire me. As I started to discuss this concept with business owners, it seemed to make sense. Would you be willing to pay a fee to meet with others like you who were also interested in helping each other? I quickly came to realize that there was a tremendous amount of skepticism in the marketplace. Many people had given up on traditional networking, and even though they commented that networking had worked for them, the sacrifices they were required to make were just not worth it.

If I did not quickly explain the six differences between Network In Action and traditional networking, the appointment was a waste of time. However, people began to realize that with great technology and professional leadership, you could get the same type of results with only a monthly 90-minute meeting. While I was out calling on businesses, Danielo was back at the office beginning to build the initial website and technology we would need to make this work. There were many evenings I retired to the house wondering if once again the market was ready for what I thought was a brilliant idea. It seemed simple to me; after all, we were trading powdered eggs for a glass of wine, a morning meeting for an afternoon engagement, rotating volunteers for professional leadership!. To top it off, we even came up with a formula that if the member participated throughout the year, we could offer them a guaranteed return on their investment.

In January 2014, we held our first meeting at Harold's in the Heights in Houston, Texas. Twenty-four business owners came together with the purpose of "building relationships that last a lifetime." There was great energy in the room, and we were creating professional networking without the drama. By having owners and decision-makers in the same room, we had created an entirely new dynamic.

Fast forward to 2020, and Network In Action is operating over 70 franchises in 18 states in our first four years of franchising. The growth has been fantastic, but we are prouder of the fact that to date, we have not had a single failure. You see, I had learned a lesson the hard way that it's one thing to go fast as we did with OurBlok and another thing to take on casualties that could take years to recover from.

I think the most important lesson I learned was to always keep people first. Ideas and concepts are great, execution is critical, but at the end of the day, for me, the relationships have to come first! The second lesson that I learned is summed up easily with a John Maxwell quote: "You are either winning or learning!" I have started over 13 businesses in 30 years, and I can assure you I have learned more from my failures than my successes. In every business I have started, it took longer to get to my initial goal, but the upside was ten times what I originally thought it would be! So, learn to enjoy the journey.

When you realize that there are roughly 4,300 franchise brands in North America and with only about 16,000 new franchises awarded annually. Your odds may be better in shark-infested waters! If my math is correct, that means, on average most brands are getting about three or four new franchise owners a year. To think that at Network In Action, we have added over 20 for three straight years gives me great gratitude.

When my wife and I started this company, we believed in our hearts, and we had a winner. We built into our franchise document a requirement that every franchise owner in the country would lead a community service project annually to help make the world a better place. Our goal was to have something going on every eight hours across the world led by our great Network In Action Franchise owners and members. We are not there yet, but today every eight days, our Network In Action groups around the country are making a meaningful contribution.

You see, at the end of the day, if you put out into the universe what's in your heart, you will get it back tenfold!

Chapter
Twenty-One

Gateway To The Arts
Audrey Walters

Audrey Walters

Talk to the Camera

Audrey Walters is a professional SAG/AFTRA actress, entrepreneur, producer, and author. In 2013, Audrey co-founded the award-winning children's program, *Talk to the Camera*, to empower the next generation through video creation and filmmaking. Talk to the Camera is a home-based franchise offering in-person and online STEAM programs for elementary-age children.

Audrey's years as a media coach and mentor at a children's talent agency fostered a passion for helping children grow creatively through on-camera work. As a premier educator for the creative spirit and visual storyteller, Audrey is passionate about fusing art and technology to inspire kids to use their imaginations.

Audrey is the producer of children's enrichment videos, *KIDS-talk*, author of the book, *Lights, Camera, Confidence*, writer and creator of the TV series, *Biological*, and Founding Media Coach at TTTC Studios. In addition, Audrey has several film and television credits, including AMC's *Better Call Saul* and Netflix Studio's *Walk. Ride. Rodeo.*

www.talktothecamera.com

audrey@talktothecamera.com

310-421-8121

By Audrey Walters

Fundamentals of Franchising

It is well understood within the franchise community that there are certain fundamentals upon which the entire industry is based. At the top of the list is the franchise business model that has been proven to be one of the most effective methods for establishing a brand, gaining market awareness, and achieving territorial distribution.

So, why are investors attracted to a franchise business model? Because it is a proven method of operation, comprehensive training and support come standard, marketing support and materials are included, and there is typically a track record of success. Most successful franchise concepts follow these similar foundational elements, but how did they get started in the beginning?

It is the entrepreneurial spark that sees a need and fills it! Then there's the hard work, persistence, and tenacity it takes to make that idea come to life. No telling who first thought up the idea of a drive-through restaurant or caring for seniors in their own homes or a flower arrangement made of fruit you eat, but they all became a franchise concept. This leads to the journey my partner, and I have been on for the past several years, as we have been perfecting our concept, Talk to the Camera.

Our Big Idea

I met Jenny Gilbert, my business partner when our kids were in preschool together. As many great relationships start, ours was an odd pairing. I'm an actor, a professional extrovert, performer, and dreamer. Jenny's a professional educator with multiple degrees, a true science- and facts-based realist.

From our first conversation, we vented about the negative impact all the small screens were having on children, in particular on our kids' social communication skills. Yes, as moms, we loved the idea of a device where kids can instantly communicate with us as well as search for information that could help in their studies. However, we both had seen the slow, creeping, and even dangerous side effects that nobody had anticipated: these devices were ruining the ability of kids to develop the social communication skills that were vital to success in life.

In dozens of classrooms over fifteen years, Jenny had seen the negative effects on her students. These kids—raised on screens—felt far more comfortable and safe connecting with a device rather than other people. Children were still curious about the world and hungry to learn, but they now lacked the confidence to speak in front of their peers.

While I had noticed the same thing with my own kids and their friends, I had also discovered, almost by accident, a way to overcome the effects of those screens: turn them the other direction and use them to build and develop social communications skills. I did it with acting.

When I met Jenny, I had been a professional working actor for several years. At the time, I was working with a child talent agency, Marbles Kids. I was teaching young kids how to act on camera, using a camera to film each performance and instantly playing it back. The kids could see how to correct negative things, like delivery and posture, but I also saw them improve their confidence during these acting/playback exercises.

Kids who want to be actors—and I'm talking kids as young as five and six—tend to come to a talent agency because their mom or dad believes in them, and the child has expressed an interest in acting. However, these kids are like all other kids: raised in part by their devices and displaying underdeveloped social communication skills. By filming these kids and playing back their performances, the kids could see how the world sees them.

They got more confident, their voices got stronger, they liked themselves more. They connected with their peers better, learned and enjoyed teamwork with other kids, and had more fun without using their devices. These kids also saw they were accomplishing things through work that was fun and rewarding. They saw that change took a little time, and those incremental changes made them stronger and better communicators.

Jenny and I were naturally very intrigued. Could this same technique work for kids who weren't actors? Could it work in a classroom setting where any kid, at any school, could improve their social communication skills with a simple camera and monitor or even the device in their hands? In short: could we turn those screens into a tool for positive growth and change for all kids?

An actress and a teacher walk into a classroom

After-school programs have come a long way since we parents were in school. Back then, most after-school activities were sports. This was fine for some kids, but not all kids are interested in sports. Could two moms with a video camera get in there and make a difference?

Like any great idea, we needed to field test it. We approached Jenny's school first since trying out a new afterschool program would be easier if it came from a licensed teacher. We had only a handful of kids that first day, and we had a complete blast!

Since I had based the concept on teaching actors at a talent agency, we had to retrofit the concept for kids looking for something fun to do after school. It couldn't be very serious since the kids at Jenny's school weren't coming to our class to become actors—they just wanted to learn how to make fun videos for YouTube.

The kids loved it, and so did the parents. Busy moms and dads told us that it was more engaging than other after-school programs. *Our* class made parents realize their kids were actually developing better face-to-face communication skills, as well as speaking up with confidence. Their kids liked the class and wanted to take it again and again!

Jenny and I had turned those screens the other direction, into something positive that helped kids grow, learn, and become more confident communicators that the modern world requires. Our program was a success and has continued to grow and evolve.

Talk to the Camera Becomes a Viable Franchise

The Talk to the Camera (TTTC) business concept had now gained popularity. And a sure sign of the need to turn your business into a franchise is when those around you begin to ask if they can get into your business themselves. A TTTC franchise business offers a fun, unique investment in today's expansive children's enrichment and visual arts industry. Our audience ranges from elementary school students taking their first course in video production, to the seasoned acting professional choosing to make a first or lasting impression on eager talent agents, producers, and directors. The TTTC brand is now being recognized in preschools, professional settings and everything in between.

From our Improv drop-in courses to our Professional Studios series, the TTTC franchise has truly become a "gateway to the arts." It serves a wide range of consumers, provides multiple streams of revenue for the franchise owner, teaches younger generations the value of audio/visual storytelling, and is a platform for professionals to enhance and promote their acting, directing, producing, and editing skills.

TTTC programs are interactive and exciting! We provide the right balance between entertainment, education, and fun to appeal to children, parents, and professionals. Our one-of-kind, award-winning programs provide tiered courses, extending the lifespan of our customers. Our students become life-long fans of our brand.

TTTC franchising provides world-class support in all aspects of our business. We have national resources for our franchisees in the form of an expansive library of school-age classroom content, legal contract templates for school district programs, well-known industry insiders as "studio" instructors, registration software, and administrative technology.

In addition, TTTC offers a variety of online virtual acting and industry-training webinars, in conjunction with advertising aimed to drive local market awareness for TTTC services. TTTC franchising also maintains a variety of proprietary relationships with prominent talent agencies in major markets, such as Los Angeles and New York City, in order to drive awareness for TTTC members within industry circles. We have a full-service marketing team, including social media experts, state-of-the-art technology, and ongoing training platforms to boost franchise owner success.

TTTC franchisees enjoy the business advantages of owning a home-based business—lower overhead costs and faster break-even time. Our franchisees enjoy being there for their families, having the flexibility to drive their kids to school while giving back to their communities by offering a program in visual arts. TTTC franchising is dedicated to supporting its franchisees. Our support is robust, and we're constantly working to ensure that our franchisees have the tools they need to thrive. We are a low cost, home-based mobile business, and we love what we do.

Owning your own franchise is a big step, and what an exciting one! With a TTTC franchise, there's the added bonus of truly making a difference and impacting the next generation. You are not only gaining an incredible business, but also a family with TTTC franchising. And if you decide we're a good fit, Jenny and I will be with you every step of the way!

Gateway to the Arts

TTTC was founded in 2013 and has been passionate about empowering kids to get creative and use their imaginations through filmmaking, being on camera and having fun. Our flagship courses for kids like, *YOUth TUBEr*, *Movie Magic*, and *News Broadcast* have been wonderful ways to help kids learn to express themselves without fear of judgment. We've seen kids blossom and grow through acting exercises, improvisation, and collaborating to make fun video projects. Kids see that they are safe to be themselves, and they often go from caterpillar to butterfly in a matter of weeks.

In 2020, TTTC made the natural shift to offering courses online with the same resounding results. Kids from all over the country began taking our award-winning courses through our virtual academy in April of 2020. Our courses became a stand-out in the online landscape, offering *live* interactive courses taught by industry professionals that are *fun*, innovative and engaging! TTTC's foundation for in-person learning translated beautifully to an online format. Today, we continue to collaborate and educate the creative spirit, the visual storyteller, and the thespian at heart.

One resounding question we received enough times to make it happen is, "Is there a TTTC for adults?" The answer is yes! Our professional courses for adults are taught by award-winning filmmakers, actors, and writers.

Where would we be today without something to watch, stream, or keep us entertained? Our world relies on stories to heal old wounds, inspire feelings of hope, teach us lessons, remind us that someone else has been in our shoes, and empowers us to believe that happily-ever-after does exist.

Imagine a world where elementary-age children are given the skillset to be confident visual content creators. Can you envision how remarkable these stories will be by the time these kids are adults? There is a need for TTTC in an ever-changing world because storytelling is a constant.

Franchisee

Chapter

Twenty-Two

Redbox+ Dumpsters Arrive In Texas

Kevin West

Kevin West

Redbox +

Kevin West has nearly 25 years of marketing and sales experience in energy and commodity-based markets. West has a record of leading functions in growth-oriented global five-hundred companies like Shell and Williams. Additionally, he consults with many large energy firms such as SunEdison, Spark Energy, TXU, Stream, EDF (France), and Engie (Germany). He has a global client base of retail energy companies.

From 2003-2009, West worked at Direct Energy, where he became Chief Marketing Officer in 2007. During his time, he guided a customer growth surge to over five million customers in North America. West oversaw the marketing activities of a broad range of products, including electricity, natural gas, renewables, air-conditioning, and home and business services. After Direct, he advanced into start-ups.

He passionately loves start-ups, having started Entrust Energy, Life Energy, and Orbit Energy based in London. He is currently working on his 12th start-up, Oeste Waste, a construction waste hauling business based in Houston, Texas, with the franchise Redbox+. His other ventures include film and photography.

Kevin has a BS in Marketing from Ball State University, an MBA from the University of Texas El Paso, and a Certificate in Energy Management from Rice University. He formerly served on the Board of Contemporary Art Museum of Fort Bend and holds an appointed position on the Fort Bend County Historical Commission since 2018.

https://www.redboxplus.com/houston-sw

kwest@redboxplus.com

281.753.9401 (C)

346.202.4811 (O)

REDBOX+ DUMPSTERS ARRIVE IN TEXAS

By Kevin Douglas West

It's been two years now since signing my Redbox+ franchise agreement, and I still wonder how I got where I am. In just 24 months, I've built a half-million-dollar business and own $850,000 in trucks and dumpsters. I have three full-time employees and two part-time seasonal workers. I'm living the American dream. I'm a serial entrepreneur—this being my 12th one. I know the hardship of starting from nothing and the thrill of seeing it turn into a tangible business with customers who need our services.

After a lucrative, 25-year corporate career in the energy industry, I found myself without a chair when the music stopped. I had left the parent company to start a new business, but resources dried up after 18 months, and we had to shut it down. I agreed with the decision despite not having my old job to go back to, but it was heartbreaking to tell our 11,000 distributors. I started consulting. That worked well for about three years, and then I decided to look for a business in existence to buy and do a turnaround. I thought this would level out my consulting cash flow.

Redbox+ is a franchise business in the waste industry. We provide dumpsters and portable toilet combination containers—and we were the first company to invent this patented product. Our franchise was the first to open in Texas, and today there are over 65 locations in the U.S. In addition to the combination containers, we also provide standard dumpsters.

Our target customers include restoration companies cleaning up after fire, water, and flood events. We also service general contractors, home builders, roofers, and demolition crews. We compete based on price and service, in addition to having our unique product to draw attention from new customer prospects.

In late 2018 I wrote my business plan and created a five-year forecast. My vision was to build a $2 million a year business with three trucks and 120 containers. My goal was to create a business that I could draw a reasonable salary from and sell in five to ten years for $1 million net. Apart from my financial objectives, I wanted to create jobs and prove to myself I can make payroll every two weeks.

My first-year investment was nearly one million, and I got off to a great start. By month three, I had already decided to nearly double my inventory of containers and buy a second truck due to the dramatic increase in business. The first two months were very slow, nothing like what the sales team thought it would be. But by month three, we were on a roll. We had more business than my one driver could handle.

Drivers are the key resource in our business. Without a driver, you cannot deliver, pickup, or discard waste. In my first year, we created two full-time driver positions and one part-time/seasonal. It's a tough job, and I hope they know how much I appreciate the contributions they make to the business. Without them, I'd have no repeat business. By the end of our second year, these drivers had delivered, picked up, and dumped 1,500 containers containing roughly 5,000 tons or ten million pounds of construction debris.

I'm roughly halfway to my goal of three full-time drivers and one dispatcher. I've handled dispatch these first years, but would eventually like to create that job. A position I didn't envision was a part-time mechanic. We've spent $60,000 this year on repairs and maintenance. I believe we can be more cost-effective with a part-time mechanic. As I continue to look for more customers, I'll need to build out more referral partners. I have one referral partner that has been truly instrumental in building our business. He came from the corporate construction industry and has a lot of contacts that he's been able to leverage into customers for us. New customers are a thrill!

It was a sunny day in mid-February, and one of the Redbox+ representatives was in town to spend a day training my driver on truck operations and then a day making sales with me. I had prepared a hit list of company targets to call on. I also wanted him to see an area within my territory that had experienced three flood events in the last two years. Those events had created a boom in rebuilding and remodeling. Homes in the area that wanted to renovate were required to raise their homes six feet. On nearly every street, there was construction activity.

We were driving around prospecting for contractors. A truck turned onto a street in front of me, and I recognized the company as a large restoration firm but didn't know anybody there. I decided to follow the truck, and when he pulled over to take a call, I parked in front of him. As soon as I saw him pull out to drive away, I jumped out of my truck and flagged him down. He rolled his window down and accepted my business card. I said I was a new company in town and would appreciate a chance to work with him. He said he'd pass along the card to someone in the office. They all say that.

But this project manager kept his word, and two days later, I got a call from the office contact in charge of vendor contracts. Within hours I was in the office pitching the business and what I could do to service their waste hauling needs. After two weeks of paperwork and insurance requirements being met, it was time to launch.

The moment I was announced as a new hauler to the 15-plus project managers in the company, my phone lit up. Calls and texts poured in and for months. We could barely keep up with the business. That first year they accounted for 70% of my revenue. Needless to say, diversification was high on my agenda for the second year. We were able to grow the business in the second year such that the restoration company was 25% of our business. They still keep us very busy, especially when flood events or fires occur.

The first two years have been full of blood, sweat, and tears. I had no idea how much working capital it would take to start a capital-intensive type of business. I've had to borrow a lot from family and draw down my retirement significantly just to get through the rough months. Insurance, gasoline, and repairs are much higher than I expected. Fortunately, margins are strong, and we can continue to get new customers at a lower cost-to-acquire. I believe there is tremendous growth potential in Houston and the entire Texas Gulf Coast area.

Like thousands upon thousands of middle-age corporate executives that leave the cushy office behind to start up a new business, my experience is probably not that dissimilar to those people. The biggest struggles include:

Lack of enough capital. This is likely the reason, so many businesses fail early. When making your financial projections, they always seem to be that sales are projected higher, and expenses are projected lower. When these two things occur, working capital flies out the door. I was lucky to have a retirement account to draw on, not that I wanted to.

Lack of enough time. There is never enough time to get everything done, especially if you continue to run other businesses or keep your day job. I started out keeping my consulting practice going but realized quickly that my franchise needed my full attention if I wanted to grow it fast and get to profitability as soon as possible. What seems to take a lot of time are permits, licenses, taxes, and never-ending forms to be completed, scanned, and filed. These tasks take you away from the sales-generating activity.

Lifestyle fit is not a match. I've been fortunate that my franchise is a perfect fit for me. I work when I need to get things done, and I take off when I want to. My business can be run 95% of the time from my phone and laptop. I do occasionally meet customers for lunch or at the jobsite, but it is rare and can be done on my own schedule. I have a small staff of drivers, so not a lot of employees to deal with. It's mostly 8:00-5:00 during the week, and only needs weekend attention in the busy stretch of summer. I never wanted to be tied to brick and mortar open/close type of business.

I've been fortunate that my wife enjoys being involved as well. We call our equipment lot "the ranch." Some people have horses or cows, we have trucks and containers. It's great to have someone able to do even the slightest of tasks when it gets so busy. She had far more reservations than I when I started. I recall the dinner where I sat down and said, "I'm going to do this business, but I want your blessing. Tell me about your reservations." She had three:

Concern over name being confused with the movie rental company. I explained I had no control over that but had confirmed the trademark was registered.

Disdain for the toilet part of the business. I stated simply, "Think of each toilet as a money-making machine." When she saw our first $20,000 check from a customer, I think that solidified in her mind.

Concern about the territory I had mapped out. Originally, I thought it would be good to buy San Antonio because when we retire, we had always talked about living in the Hill Country. I thought, ten years working in San Antonio, then retire nearby. But her concern was the travel. She knows when I start something new, I tend to jump all the way in and that I'd be traveling to San Antonio every week, spending a couple nights building the business. I gave in on this one and mapped a territory in southwest Houston, where we live. She was right. Knowing now what it's taken to build this, I would have been gone 100 nights a year, and that wouldn't have been good for our relationship. Especially given the strain of building a new business without traveling.

At the end of our dinner, she kissed me and said, "All right, we're in the toilet business." I'm the luckiest guy in the world to have a spouse that supports me on my journey despite the big change of lifestyle we've endured to do this. In the build-phase, there are no luxury vacations, new cars, or steak dinners with expensive wine. It's Holiday Inn Express with free breakfast when we have to travel, cars with over 200,000 miles, and beans and rice for dinner at home!

If you are thinking of owning a franchise, my single most important piece of advice is to read the entire franchise agreement and then have an attorney review it. Your attorney will find 20-plus things to talk to you about in the agreement, but you will be wiser for it. There will be things they recommend that are changed, but the franchisor won't budge on any of them. However, they might concede a few things in an addendum. After that, you are on your own, and those loan payments will hit the 15th of every month for the next 60 months, so get out and hustle right away and never stop.

I've helped many entrepreneurs build businesses, but this is my first capital-intensive start-up all on my own. It might be my last big business hurrah. I doubt it. Something else will come in my range and draw me in. But for now, I'm proud of where we've gotten to and look forward to building my legacy business! It's time for the next phase of capital infusion and growth. This next phase includes new types of investors and lenders and, most importantly, a new level of customer type and sales channels.

So, if you currently find yourself contemplating franchise ownership, I say dive in headfirst. Work like you've never worked before, and don't give up.

The good days will eventually outweigh the bad ones!

"The way to get started is to quit talking and start doing." ~ Walt Disney, Co-Founder, Disney

www.ingramcontent.com/pod-product-compliance
Lightning Source LLC
LaVergne TN
LVHW010054110826
845155LV00028B/332

* 9 7 8 1 9 5 1 1 3 1 1 5 9 *